RESOURCE BOOKS FOR TEACHERS

series editor

ALAN MALEY

GRAMMAR DICTATION

Ruth Wajnryb

Oxford University Press

Oxford University Press
Great Clarendon Street, Oxford OX2 6DP

Oxford New York
Athens Auckland Bangkok Bogotá Buenos Aires
Calcutta Cape Town Chennai Dar es Salaam
Delhi Florence Hong Kong Istanbul Karachi
Kuala Lumpur Madrid Melbourne Mexico City
Mumbai Nairobi Paris São Paulo Shanghai
Singapore Taipei Tokyo Toronto Warsaw

and associated companies in
Berlin Ibadan

Oxford and *Oxford English* are trade marks of Oxford University Press

ISBN 0 19 437004 6

© Oxford University Press 1990

First published 1990
Ninth impression 2001

Set by Pentacor Ltd, High Wycombe, Bucks

Printed in China

Acknowledgements

I wish to thank the teachers at Sydney English Language Centre.

To the memory of Nelly Wajnryb

Contents

Activity	*Topic*	*Structural focus*	
Section 1: pre-intermediate			
1.1 Marco Polo	Famous people Travelling	Past simple tense Prepositions: *from, to, about*	26
1.2 Earthquake	Natural disasters	Past simple tense Existential *there* Simple sentence structure Prepositional phrases	27
1.3 World English	English Language and communication	Present simple tense *Some* and *others* as pronouns Textual reference Gerunds	28
1.4 I'm Kate	Self-identification	Contractions Present simple tense Present perfect simple tense showing duration (*for*) Gerund after *like* Adverbial intensifier (*really*)	29
1.5 Dear diary	Diaries	Past simple tense Conjunctions: *and, because, so* Adverbs of degree: *too* and *very* Zero article Contractions Prepositions: *on* + weekday	30
1.6 Garlic, the great healer	Health and medicine	Time expressions Present perfect simple tense Past simple tense Causal connections	32
1.7 Child mother	Human interest story	Present perfect simple tense Past simple tense *Of* and *'s* genitives Adjectives	33

Section 3: advanced

The author and series editor

Ruth Wajnryb is a professional teacher trainer and materials writer. She has a MA in Applied Linguistics from Sydney University with research in the area of error analysis and language-learner language. She has worked as the Director of teacher training and professional development at a number of institutes and colleges in Sydney. Her work has included both pre-service training of language teachers and professional development of teachers. She has over twenty years' experience in the field of adult education in Australia, England, Israel and South America. She is currently engaged in doctoral research into the language of supervision in the context of TESOL teacher education.

She is the author of *Grammar Workout, Grammar Workout 2, Profiles, Afterthoughts, Other Voices,* and *Classroom Observation Tasks.*

Alan Maley worked for the British Council from 1962 to 1988, serving as English Language Officer in Yugoslavia, Ghana, Italy, France, and China, and as Regional Representative for The British Council in South India (Madras). From 1988 to 1993 he was Director-General of the Bell Educational Trust, Cambridge. He is currently Senior Fellow in the Department of English Language and Literature of the National University of Singapore. He has written *Literature*, in this series, *Beyond Words, Sounds Interesting, Sounds Intriguing, Words, Variations on a Theme,* and *Drama Techniques in Language Learning* (all with Alan Duff), *The Mind's Eye* (with Françoise Grellet and Alan Duff), *Learning to Listen* and *Poem into Poem* (with Sandra Moulding), and *Short and Sweet.* He is also Series Editor for the Oxford Supplementary Skills series.

Foreword

Grammar Dictation differs somewhat from other books in this series. Rather than offering a range of different techniques or activities focused on a particular area of interest, it presents one central idea which is exemplified in a large number of concrete instances.

It does, nevertheless, offer teachers a significant resource (rather than a course). The materials can be used flexibly to suit different groups at different stages of their development. Further, teachers can build upon this resource by applying the procedure to texts of their own choosing.

'Grammar dictation' is better known in some quarters as the 'dictogloss' procedure. Essentially it consists of asking learners to reconstruct a dictated text so as to capture as much as possible of its information content in as accurate and acceptable a linguistic form as possible.

This process requires learners to draw upon a nexus of interrelated skills. Initially learners engage individually in the creative reconstruction of text from memory and from their own linguistic resources. They then share this with others in a process of gradual approximation to a final product. With time and practice they learn to refine and develop their own linguistic resources but always in relation to what they already know. The contribution of individual and group effort are nicely balanced.

The approach is especially interesting for the way it reconciles certain apparent oppositions such as the new interest in grammar and the need for interactive learning; and the achievement of accuracy through fluency activities. The final product is important (in part as input to further analysis), but the individual and group process is integral in moulding and shaping it. Individual learner perceptions of wants are reconciled with teacher perceptions of learner needs.

Grammar Dictation offers teachers and learners a powerful and effective tool for learning. We recommend you try it.

Alan Maley

Introduction

Grammar dictation and dictogloss

The title *Grammar Dictation* describes a language teaching
procedure known in those areas of the world where it is already
extensively used, as 'dictogloss' or 'the dictogloss procedure'.

Since many teachers may not be very familiar with the procedure, it
was felt that the title *Dictogloss* might prove somewhat awesome.
The title *Grammar Dictation* contains two of the basic ingredients of
the dictogloss procedure. As you work your way through this book,
you will discover others.

However, for practical purposes the term 'grammar dictation' and
'dictogloss' are used synonymously.

What is dictogloss?

Dictogloss is a relatively recent procedure in language teaching. It
borrows a little from traditional dictation (hence part of its name)
but in fact is quite distinct from dictation in both procedure and
objectives. In dictogloss, a short text is read at normal speed to a
class of learners who jot down familiar words as they listen. At the
end of the dictation stage, most learners have only a small number
of isolated words (or fragments) which together make up a very
incohesive, 'battered text'. In small groups, the students then pool
their resources to reconstruct their version of the original text. In
the final stage the various versions that the students have produced
are subjected to close analysis and comparison. Through both the
task of reconstruction and the following error analysis, students
refine their understanding of the language they have used.

The procedure may be summarized as follows:

a. A short, dense text is read (twice) to the learners at normal speed
b. As it is being read, the learners jot down familiar words and
   phrases
c. Working in small groups, the learners pool their battered texts
   and strive to reconstruct a version of the text from their shared
   resources
d. Each group of students produces its own reconstructed version,
   aiming at grammatical accuracy and textual cohesion but not at
   replicating the original text

e. The various versions are analysed and compared and the students refine their own texts in the light of the shared scrutiny and discussion.

The resemblance of dictogloss to traditional dictation is only superficial. The analogy begins and ends with the fact that in both a passage is dictated. In dictogloss the style of dictating, the focus on a text approach to grammar, the task that follows, and the objective of the lesson are all totally different. Here the learners are obliged to create their own parallel texts. These are semantic approximations to the original text, created out of the learners' own grammatical and linguistic resources.

Dictogloss is a task-based procedure designed to help language-learning students towards a better understanding of how grammar works on a text basis. It is designed to expose where their language-learner shortcomings (and needs) are, so that teaching can be directed more precisely towards these areas. In this sense it is eminently learner-needs based.

Who is this book designed for?

This book is designed to help improve the student's understanding and use of grammar. It is addressed to the teachers of learners whose primary needs are:

– a more precise understanding of how to use the grammar of English
– accuracy in language use for both spoken and written purposes
– written English, for example, at school, college, or university, where students are required to write cohesive texts in English (such as essays, assignments, reports, theses)
– preparation for entrance examinations to institutes of higher education where a knowledge of grammar and the ability to write a sustained piece of prose are required.

Aims

Dictogloss has a number of aims:

a. It aims to provide an opportunity for learners to use their productive grammar in the task of text creation. Learners' linguistic resources are called upon as they pool their fragmented notes and consider the various language options available to them.
b. It aims to encourage learners to find out what they do and do not know about English. This is realized in the attempts to reconstruct the text and in the subsequent analysis of those attempts.

c. It aims to upgrade and refine the learners' use of the language through a comprehensive analysis of language options in the correction of the learners' approximate texts.

Learners who regularly engage in dictogloss lessons will gradually see a refinement in their global aural comprehension and note-taking skills. While these are not primary aims of the method, they are important by-products of it.

What happens in the dictogloss procedure?

There are four stages in the procedure:

1 Preparation, when the learner finds out about the topic of the text and is prepared for some of the vocabulary.

2 Dictation, when the learner hears the text and takes fragmentary notes.

3 Reconstruction, when the learner reconstructs the text on the basis of the fragments recorded in stage 2.

4 Analysis and correction, when learners analyse and correct their texts.

The four stages of dictogloss

1 Preparation

At this first stage, teachers should:

a. Prepare learners for the text they will be hearing by exploiting the warm-up suggestions in each lesson. This type of topical warm-up prepares learners for the subject matter and makes them more receptive to the listening in the next stage: people listen more effectively when they are able to anticipate what they will hear, when their interest in the topic has been aroused, and when they become personally involved in the discussion.

b. Prepare learners for the vocabulary of the text. The list in each unit is a suggestion only. Vocabulary should be pre-taught if the teacher suspects that it is unknown to the learners or difficult for them to infer.

c. Ensure that learners know what they are expected to do at each stage of the procedure.

d. Organize learners into groups before the dictation begins.

2 Dictation

As a standard procedure, learners should hear the dictation twice. The first time, they should not write, but allow the words to 'wash over them'. This way they get a global feeling for the whole passage. The second time, they should take down notes.

When the students take notes during the dictation, they should be encouraged to write down the type of word that will help them to piece together the text in the later reconstruction stage. Such words are content or information words, for example, *farmer*, *sold*, *horse*, that serve as memory cues or triggers. The grammar or function words, for example, *the*, *his*, *and*, are to be provided by the learners themselves as part of the productive process of reconstructing the text.

The text should be dictated at normal spoken speed. The general pace is comparable to that of a news broadcast on radio or TV. The dictating should not be conducted in the traditional way where the sentence is broken up into isolated word units. The semantic grouping here is the sentence. Between sentences, the pauses should be slightly longer than usual; a brisk count to five under one's breath is a good standard. As far as is possible the two readings should be identical.

3 Reconstruction

As soon as the dictation is finished, the learners, working in groups, proceed to pool their notes and work on their version of the text. It helps if each group has a 'scribe' through whom all suggestions are channelled. The scribe writes down the group's text as it emerges from group discussion. When it is complete, the group checks the text for grammar, textual cohesion, and logical sense.

The teacher's role during reconstruction is to monitor the activity but not to provide any actual language input. However, to facilitate the error analysis/correction stage to follow, it sometimes helps to pre-empt the problem of 'error clutter'. If a group's text is too cluttered with grammatical errors, it is difficult in stage 4 to focus attention on the areas of primary need. To prevent this, the teacher in the reconstruction stage should point out minor peripheral errors to learners while they are still drafting their texts. In other words, the teacher may unobtrusively contribute to the group's 'conferencing'. If a text has been chosen for its structural language point (for example past tenses) then the errors to be eliminated in the drafting stage would be in areas other than this, for example, articles or prepositions. This helps to clear the path so that the final error analysis can focus clearly on the main point of the lesson.

Expressed another way, the learners should not be stopped from committing errors in the chosen structural area, and peripheral errors should be cleared up, so that learning in the final stage of analysis and correction can be more concentrated and effective.

More guidance about the learner's role during the reconstruction stage is included in the section below: *Immediate task objectives*.

4 Analysis and correction

The last stage of the dictogloss procedure is the analysis and correction of the learners' texts. There are various ways of conducting this. Teachers will conduct this session in their own preferred fashion.

a. Using the blackboard, the students' texts are written up for all to see and discuss. This is best conducted on a sentence basis – sentence 1 of each group is analysed before moving on to sentence 2 of each group.

b. Instead of the blackboard, an overhead projector can be used.

c. Each text can be photocopied and the class can examine them, either as a total unit or on a sentence-by-sentence basis. If a sentence base is preferred, then it helps to cut and paste the texts into sentence groupings before photocopying.

d. Another technique (which can accompany any of the correction ideas listed here) is to keep a copy of the original text (as dictated) on an overhead projector and to 'scroll' it forward sentence by sentence after the students' versions have been examined.

Whichever correction procedure the teacher selects, students should be encouraged to compare the various versions and discuss the language choices made. In this way errors are exposed and discussed so that learners understand the hypotheses, false and otherwise, that underlie their choices. Ideally, the original text should not be seen by learners until after their own versions have been analysed.

Immediate task objectives

In the reconstruction stage, a group of learners should have in mind two immediate goals or objectives:

a. To maintain as much information as possible from the original text.

b. To produce a sound English text.

Maintaining informational content

In the reconstruction stage learners pool their fragments. These are not really notes in the note-taking sense of information that has been decoded, processed, and reassembled. They are merely bits or fragments of language written down as heard during the dictation. Groups should aim to maintain the informational content of the original. For example, take the sentence: 'The man in the grey suit carrying the black umbrella walked into the shop.' If this sentence were reconstructed by students to read 'The man walked into the shop,' then it is clear that it omits some of the original information. It should be noted, however, that the students' texts do not have to replicate the original. Continuing with the same example, the following reconstruction is perfectly acceptable: 'The man who was wearing a grey suit and carrying a black umbrella walked into the shop.' There are, of course, other versions that would be equally acceptable.

Producing a sound English text

The text produced should be sound in three senses. Firstly, it should be grammatically accurate, abiding by syntactic and structural rules of English usage. Secondly, it should be textually cohesive. This means it should hold together as a unit or chunk of language that is meaningful as an integral whole. A five-sentence text has a tight logical sequence; it is not a loose random collection of individual sentence-units. The use of connectives between sentences and of reference devices to interconnect ideas is crucial here. Thirdly, the text produced should make logical sense in terms of our knowledge of the real world. An example will clarify this. The sentence: 'The American University in Beirut is the oldest institution in the Arab world' is out of kilter with what we know about the world, and so it is illogical even while being structurally accurate.

Interaction

The key to the dictogloss approach to grammar is interaction. The method requires learners in the classroom to interact with each other in small groups so as to reconstruct the text as a co-operative endeavour. Working in this way, learners are actively engaged in the learning process. Through active learner involvement students come to confront their own strengths and weaknesses in English language use. In so doing, they find out what they do not know, then they find out what they need to know. It is through this process that they improve their language skills.

Teaching with dictogloss

In teaching with dictogloss, teachers should remember that the aim is to develop learners' grammatical competence in using the language. The procedure is a very specific one, although teachers will inevitably introduce variations that suit their own teaching styles and situations. With experience, students become familiar with the procedure and the phases become predictable parts of a familiar process. As students realize that they are learning and that their English is developing, their confidence in both learning and using the language increases.

Further information about dictogloss

The interested reader is referred to the *Bibliography* section of this book, which contains a list of articles that have been written on various aspects of dictogloss.

What is the value of dictogloss?

Learning is active involvement

As they learn, students make many and varied and constantly changing hypotheses about language. These involve the learner in active decision-making about the target language. Some of these decisions are conscious, some subconscious; some relate to learning, some to communication strategies. The hypotheses are tested out and the results of each test – the feedback – are processed by the learner who then adjusts a current hypothesis to accommodate the new data received. As a consequence, learning means constant flux: the language of the language learner is always changing and this very instability is a sign of progress. Each adjustment to the learner's 'interlanguage' sees a closer approximation to the target language. In this way, learners edge their way towards the ultimate goal, which is mastery of the systems of the target language.

This approach to language learning underpins the dictogloss approach. By being task-based it allows learners to try out the language, that is, to try out their hypotheses and subsequently receive more data about the language. The error analysis and correction stage provides an almost immediate source of feedback, which itself allows learners to make the appropriate adjustments to their understanding of how the target language is governed.

Teaching while testing

Dictogloss offers a unique blending of the twin functions of testing and teaching. The testing function acts as a means of diagnosing the learners' current language understanding. In each dictogloss lesson, learners find out a little about what they know and do not know in the target language. In the reconstruction stage, specifically in the group effort to create a text, learners expand their understanding of what options exist and are available to them in the language. In the error analysis and correction stage, learners consolidate their understanding of which options are the most suitable. What dictogloss offers, then, is an integrated 'package' of testing and teaching, incorporating both a free, experimental stage as well as more guided and structured learning. The interactive relationship between the 'teach' and 'test' elements is a key factor in its success.

An information gap – the role of memory and creativity

In dictogloss, a pivotal balance exists between the role of memory and the role of creativity. For the procedure to work effectively, this balance must be understood and, indeed, exploited. Essentially, at the moment when learners begin the text reconstruction, they are faced with a central and crucially important 'information gap'. This is the gap which exists between, on the one hand, learners' 'knowledge-to-date' of the text (what they remember plus what they have noted down during the dictation), and on the other hand, the task to be completed, that is, the reconstruction of a semantic unit of language that is grammatically sound and textually cohesive.

Thus, at the beginning of the reconstruction stage, learners are in a position where they lack enough data to reproduce with ease the text to which they have been exposed. This is, of course, entirely intentional. The text is dense. It is dictated quickly. Learners are exposed to it aurally, not visually. As a result, the fragments that the learners collect are insufficient to allow them to reconstruct the text effortlessly. They are therefore obliged to call on their pre-existing knowledge of language – their grammatical competence – to see them through the task.

This, then, is the gap that compels the learners to activate what they know of the language in order to perform the task. What they produce in the end is not a replica of the original text, but this was never the intention. They produce in fact a 'gloss' (a paraphrase in their own words) of the original text, something that is in a very real sense an original work.

Grammar in context

The issue of grammar is approached from within the context in which that grammar is found. In other words, language forms, structures, and patterns are treated from the perspective of their particular contextual meaning. They are not dealt with in isolation as instances of rules where usage is devoid of a semantic base. This is as it should be. Grammar that is disembodied from a context has little meaning or practical value for the language learner.

In both the reconstruction stage and the error analysis stage of dictogloss, the issue of grammar is approached contextually. In the reconstruction stage, learners are required to perform a very specific, context-based task. Using their pooled notes, the aid that short-term memory provides, and, most importantly, their knowledge of the language, they (re)construct a text whose topic, point of view, and parameters are already known. In other words, the context is predetermined: it is firmly established prior to the reconstruction stage. In this way, learners' grammatical construct is fitted into the already-established context.

In the final stage, that of error analysis and correction, once again the approach is contextually anchored. The various text versions that the groups of learners produce are treated in terms of the given context. The options are then considered, debated, and selected totally within the framework of their linguistic and situational context.

A compromise between traditional and contemporary approaches to learning grammar

Dictogloss addresses and tries to resolve a central conflict at the heart of language teaching today. This conflict relates to the question of grammar, its role in language learning, and its place in the classroom. The grammar problem itself hinges on two main issues. The first issue involves the perception of needs; the second, connected to the first, is a question of teaching methodology.

The first area of conflict is the difference between how the learner perceives his or her needs and how the teacher perceives those needs. Where, happily, there is agreement, there is no problem. Too often, however, there is little or no agreement. Often the learner thinks (and states) that 'the problem is grammar'. It is not difficult to understand how this opinion is formed. Grammar is what most learners think language is. If there is a problem with learning the language, then it must indicate a need for more grammar.

Often, though, the problem has nothing to do with grammar. It might have far more to do with the socio-cultural domain than with the correct sequence of tenses. Or it may be that the learners need very specific training in a particular micro-skill – (listening for gist, or listening for specific information); or that they might want more opportunity for fluency practice in communicative contexts.

Such needs cannot be solved by increasing the grammar input. The teacher might know this; but it is often the case that the learner does not. When the teacher perceives the learner's needs to be different from those that the learner perceives – that is, when the teacher's diagnosis does not match up with the learner's self-diagnosis – then there is potential for conflict and frustration in both the learning and teaching processes.

Even if the teacher and learner could reach some agreement on the question of needs, there still remains the problem of agreeing on the management or treatment of these needs. Here we have another source of potential conflict, the question of methodology. Many are the learners who want 'grammar lessons', and by this they usually mean five rules for the use of the present perfect simple tense, or six rules for the use of the definite article. These days, when greater emphasis in teaching falls on language as communication, and when more and more teachers would describe themselves as 'communicative', fewer teachers are prepared to give traditional lessons on the rules of usage.

This leaves us with a problem. Learners want grammar lessons and teachers are increasingly loath to provide them. We could override our learners' clamours with a patronizing and dismissive 'we know best'. However, more and more we are coming to realize that a methodology that violates the learners' preferred learning style will be of little value to them in the long run.

It is at this seeming impasse that dictogloss comes into the picture. Dictogloss is a working compromise. It meets students and teachers half-way and avoids 'bitter pills' being swallowed by either. It is a compromise between what the learners think they want (grammar) and what the teachers want to give them (communicative practice in a task-based, learner-centred context). It gives learners what they think they want, and what in fact they may need, but it does so in a manner that most teachers find palatable, that does not violate more traditional preferred learning styles, that is consistent with contemporary thinking in applied linguistics, and that accommodates recent trends in language teaching.

Motivation

Dictogloss is grammar in response to visible needs – not dry, remote, and removed as so much grammar teaching tends to be.

Few would deny that learners are most motivated to learn when they consider that the teaching to which they are being exposed is pitched to meet their individual needs. Moreover, learners expect teachers to provide them with the sort of feedback that throws light on the correctness as well as the appropriateness of the language options they have made.

By integrating the functions of testing and teaching, dictogloss helps to stimulate the learners' motivation. The procedure allows the learners 'to try their hand' so to speak (the reconstruction stage); the teaching phase is then based on the analysis of the learners' errors (the correction stage). It is not a question of the teacher's deciding, say, 'This class needs work on articles; I'll give them a lesson on that'. Rather, the teacher provides a task that requires a knowledge of article usage and then, guided by manifest learner error, teaches the students in response to their need.

All my language teaching experience confirms the twin notions that learners want and need error correction, and that teaching which caters for individual error cashes in handsomely on student motivation.

Another factor worthy of consideration is the relationship of the group process to individual motivation. When learners offer their contribution to the group in the context of the reconstruction stage, they are making a commitment – to the group, to the task, and to the learning process.

Inevitably, they will be affected by how the group responds to their efforts and energies, and by how the teacher (in the correction stage) responds to their group's efforts. A positive learning climate in the group is something that the teacher can subtly engineer, essentially by pre-emptive action: by carefully selecting the groups; by selecting the group's 'scribe'; by closely, if unobtrusively, monitoring the groups' interaction. The final stage of error analysis and correction again is something that should be conducted to maximize learning and encourage risk-taking. All this in effect means that the dictogloss procedure can capitalize on learners' willingness to learn and allow the teacher to maintain learner motivation at a high and effective level.

The experiential factor

If one thing has successfully emerged from the last decade of language teaching, it is the experiential factor. Learners learn best by the activity of doing, by trying out language, by being actively engaged in tasks that have been carefully designed to generate specific language patterns.

We have abandoned as invalid the 'receptacle' approach, where language is perceived as a body of knowledge to be imbibed, and the teacher is perceived as the imparter of this 'informational package'. This approach works on a deficiency assumption – there is a hole, and you fill it up.

Language is now seen as communication, as a vehicle of socio-cultural expression and interaction. Language teaching is understood to be the creation of valid learning contexts and climates. These are the lessons learned from the last decade.

On an experiential level, dictogloss is an ideal vehicle for active learning. The core component of the procedure is the student-completed task of the reconstruction stage. Here learners are engaged in the process of creative construction of language in the form of a short text. Their texts subsequently became the basis of analysis and scrutiny as a result of which a deeper understanding of the target language is facilitated.

The individual and the group

Dictogloss caters for learners both as individuals and as members of a group. The learner as an individual is catered for because the working groups are small enough to allow for individual contributions to be incorporated into the group effort. Careful selection of groups as well as time allowed to complete the task of reconstruction – these are the ingredients that best allow the individuals to make their mark on the group and feel rewarded for their efforts.

The beauty of dictogloss, however, is that even while allowing for individual contribution, in a sense the group provides a protective shield to cushion the egos of the individuals so that they are not threatened as people. The analysis of the texts in the final stage is conducted on the groups' versions, thereby extending a certain protective anonymity to each member, so that they can capitalize on the error correction without feeling personally responsible, ashamed, or losing face in front of their peers.

Communication and group interaction

The central feature of dictogloss is that it is task based, as seen in the reconstruction stage. Here a small group of learners co-operates as a team by sharing their resources to carry out the task. The essence of this stage, then, is learner involvement and interaction.

Group work is therefore crucial to the approach. It is appropriate, then, to consider in some degree of depth the exact place and value of group work in the language classroom:

1 We should consider the part language plays in thought process, and the value of using language to thrash things out, in preference to asking individuals to 'problem-solve' silently. This touches, too, on the relationship between learners' active and passive knowledge of the target language and on how talking to each other can serve to trigger and activate knowledge and competence that otherwise might lie dormant and relatively untapped. Recalling the cognitive base of language learning on which dictogloss draws, the fact that a small group of learners is placed in a situation of verbal interaction and involvement means that in a sense their various hypotheses about the target language have to be voiced. Being voiced, these hypotheses become clearer and more conscious to the learner; as

such, they are therefore more manageable and ultimately more remediable.

2 The inclusion of group work means that there is greater intensity of language involvement. More learners are using more language in the same amount of time compared to a more teacher-centred style of teaching. This means that the quality of language practice is also increased, since the opportunities for feedback, learner-initiated repair, and monitoring are all enhanced. This in turn has a positive effect on learner motivation.

3 While the quantity of talk is being increased, so too is its quality. The primary point here is the group's communicative raison d'être. The learners need to use language in order to complete their task; hence their reason for interacting is genuine and not 'display-based' or teacher-constructed. One might argue, in fact, that in this case the interaction may be more important than the result of the interaction. This means that 'the hidden curriculum' of interaction, exchange, negotiation, discussion, repair, and compromise may actually be more important in the learning process than the actual production of the reconstructed text.

4 A point related to the quality of interaction in a genuine communication setting is the fact that the context of face-to-face exchange that a group offers is indeed a far more natural setting for conventional interaction than the traditional whole-class situation. The type of interaction engaged in itself more closely simulates 'real' conversation – that is, personalized, creative talk. It therefore offers the opportunity for many of the sorts of roles, functions, and skills for which we are preparing learners in the EFL/ESL classroom. In these terms, traditional, full-classroom discourse in the 'lock-step' mode – with a single distant initiator (the teacher) and a group interlocutor (the learners) – is quite unnatural. Not only does the small-group setting reduce the stress of public performance; it provides an appropriate environment for linguistically natural behaviour. Learners co-operating in groups are not limited to producing hurried, isolated sentences; but rather, can engage in cohesive and coherent sequences of utterances, thereby developing discourse competence, not just (at best) a sentence grammar.

5 By moving away from the lock-step rhythm of whole-class organization, group work assists individualization. Each group in a sense is unique, being both strengthened and limited by its own capabilities. It finds its own individual working pace, which reflects and accommodates its members rather than the exigencies of the whole class, where the lock-step is often allowed to ride roughshod over individual differences. Allowed to work at its own pace, a group therefore is able to develop greater autonomy and independence. The benefits of such reduced teacher-dependence should produce spin-off outside the classroom.

6 Another factor is related to this question of greater individualization. Classroom organization in the form of group work allows for the development of a small learning community which provides support for the voicing of individual contributions as well as lending such individual contributions a comforting degree of anonymity (see *The individual and the group*, above). There is also the factor of group responsibility for the work produced. As a group pools its resources to perform the task of reconstruction of the dictogloss text, they assume common ownership of the version they are creating. This inevitably generates a certain pride of ownership and increases learners' commitment to their energy investment.

7 The creation of small learning communities means increased participation and learner co-operation. This injection of 'democracy' into the classroom allows learners to complement each others' strengths and weaknesses.

8 A further point relates to the affective climate of the classroom. Group work reduces the stress on the learner (as well as the teacher) by moving interaction away from the public arena. This improves the group dynamic, which itself allows for the phenomenon of 'exploratory talk' among peers, something which is rendered impossible by the size, power asymmetry, and lack of intimacy of the full classroom. In exploratory talk, the learner is allowed to focus on the meaning rather than the form of the spoken message. With the pressure taken off accuracy, and the inhibition of being monitored removed, the learner is thus allowed greater freedom to explore aloud and so to use language as a non-learner would use it.

9 A last point needs to be made regarding the nature of student talk in the information-gap type of interaction. In such interactions, the level of accuracy of student production has been found to be as high as in teacher-monitored work. At the same time, the quality of negotiation and repair in interlanguage talk has been significantly higher than in teacher-fronted, whole-class settings.

In the light of these considerations on the value of group work and how it relates to dictogloss, it would seem clear that the type and quality of interlanguage talk engaged in by learners reconstructing a dictogloss text is such as to enhance the quality of their language learning.

The text as the unit of language

The foundation stone of dictogloss is the concept of text. Text provides the point of departure from which the procedure begins (the dictation); it is the goal towards which the learners direct their energies (the reconstruction); and it is the framework within which their efforts are measured (the analysis). It may be said, then, that a basic premise of the whole procedure is the value placed on text as the semantic unit of language.

Having as its base unit the text (rather than the sentence or the word), means that the learner is compelled to consider the concept of text as a unit at every stage, from the dictation, through the reconstruction to the analysis. The fact that text is the semantic unit from which language is approached, means that textual considerations are brought into being in both the decoding of language (dictation) and in its encoding (reconstruction). Dictogloss puts great emphasis on the cross-sentence connections, as well as all the various means – notably, reference, ellipsis, and substitution – by which textual cohesion is established and maintained in English.

In addition, there is the sense of the text as culture-specific, in this case to English. By this I mean that they each offer a linguistic way of ordering experiences, a world view that is uniquely English. Language is, of course, culture-specific, and in the textual organization of each of these models lies a cultural basis the understanding of which has great value for the language learner. Continued and regular exposure to and construction of these characteristic text-types will facilitate the language-learner's understanding, appreciation, and manipulation of the logical and rhetorical world of English. For those learners whose first language rests on a very different logic system or world view, this is enormously important and valuable.

How to use this book

How the book is organized

This book contains 60 texts for use in dictogloss lessons. It is organized into three sections divided according to level. Each section contains 20 dictogloss texts. Section 1 has 20 texts at the pre-intermediate level, ranging from elementary to post-elementary. These are numbered 1.1–1.20. Section 2 contains 20 texts at the intermediate level, graded from low intermediate to upper intermediate and numbered 2.1–2.20. Section 3 contains 20 texts at the advanced level, numbered 3.1–3.20 and the texts here range from lower advanced to very advanced.

There are two indexes at the end of the book. One is a thematic index containing an alphabetical index of topics, themes, and issues that form the subject of the texts. This is designed to assist teachers who wish the text to fit in with other material in the teaching programme.

The second is a structural index with an alphabetical list of the key structures of the texts. This is designed to help teachers who are choosing a text to teach or consolidate a grammar point.

Teachers are advised to consult the section *Adjusting the level of a text* to help them exploit a text that is thematically or structurally appropriate but at the wrong level for the class for which it is intended.

How each activity is organized

Each text is the basis of a dictogloss lesson. The lesson is organized into a number of key areas to assist the teacher: *Topic*, *Language points*, *Preparation Warm-up*, *Pre-text vocabulary*, *Text*, *Notes*.

Topic
This refers to the subject matter, theme, or area of interest that the text deals with.

Language points
These state the key grammatical points that form the structural focus of the text.

Preparation
This refers to anything you occasionally need to prepare before going into the classroom.

Warm-up

These are suggestions for ways to 'enter' the lesson or prepare the learners for the topic of the text they are about to hear.

Pre-text vocabulary

This is a short list of words that you may need to introduce to the learners before the text is heard. The aim is to avoid the learners hearing any unfamiliar words for the first time in the dictation. You should adjust the pre-text vocabulary list according to what you know of your students.

Text

This is the dictogloss text that is dictated to the learners. The sentences are numbered to facilitate reading and reference. The students should not see the text until the final stage of the dictogloss procedure, when they have listened to it, taken down notes, and reconstructed their own version. Ideally, too, the correction stage should be conducted with the focus on the students' texts rather than on the original text.

Notes

These are notes on the grammar of the text designed to assist in the analysis and correction stage.

It should be pointed out that the grammatical notes are meant to address the needs of a wide range of teachers, from the beginning teacher who requires not only information about language but also a language to talk about language; to the more experienced and language-aware teacher who will select notes as required. The notes do not claim to be exhaustive, for such is the nature and complexity of language and language learning that one cannot hope to predict every language option that learners may produce. However, the notes are designed to cater for the most common types of structural and textual problems that arise.

For further clarification of grammatical terms the reader is referred to the language terminology section at the beginning of Swan: *Practial English Usage*, Oxford University Press, 1980.

There is no mention made in the lesson outlines of aims/objectives, procedural steps, timing, or the appropriate age of the learner. These have been omitted from the lesson outlines as they remain virtually constant throughout the book. The aims and objectives of the dictogloss procedure, as set out in the *Introduction* to the book, do not change through the three sections, as they are not dependent on level. Likewise, the procedure remains constant, irrespective of the level of the learner. The timing factor is broadly the same, and guidelines for this are offered below. With regard to the age of the target learner, dictogloss is suitable for young adults upwards (that is, 15+) but is certainly not appropriate for younger children learning a second or foreign language.

More guidelines for teachers

Timing

The amount of time spent depends partly on how familiar students are with the method. As they become more familiar with it, it involves less time. The primary factor, however, in determining the length of time to be spent is how much attention you and the students wish to devote to the analysis and correction stage.

Guideline to time allocation:

Stage	Activity	Time
1	Preparation	20 minutes
2	Dictation	5 minutes
3	Reconstruction	30 minutes
4	Analysis, correction, discussion	30–45 minutes

Selecting a text

There are three primary criteria for the selection of a text:

Level
You may choose a text suitable to the level of the students. The texts are carefully graded so that the early ones cater for elementary and then pre-intermediate students, while the later ones are more appropriate for post-intermediate and advanced learners.

Theme
You may wish to consider the thematic relevance of a text in relation to the students' interests and the ongoing teaching programme.

Language points
Each text highlights specific language and textual points that can serve as a teaching focus.

The two indexes at the back of the book should help you to select the right text for your classes.

Adjusting the level of a text

It may be that you will want to select a text for its thematic or structural focus, but find the level inappropriate. There are a number of ways in which the level of a text can be modified to suit a particular group of learners. These adjustments (listed below) affect the ease of accessibility learners have to a text.

You can adjust:
- the amount of preparation and prediction in the pre-dictation stage
- the amount of vocabulary that is pre-taught

- the number of times the text is dictated
- the speed of the dictation, including the length of the pauses between sentences.

In these ways the texts can be made either more or less accessible to the learners. Your decisions here will depend on your knowledge of the learners' level of English. The point cannot be emphasized enough that at no level are learners expected to be able to note down all or even most of the text heard (as in traditional dictation). Were they able to do this, then the task of reconstruction would be perfunctory and pedagogically pointless. By having only some fragments of a battered text, they are thereby compelled into creativity and construction. It is the task and the analysis of the task that makes for the learning potential here. (As an incidental, but related point, if learners have insufficient notes to put together one of the sentences, they should be encouraged to make it up completely, taking into consideration both topical and textual considerations.)

Grading, level, and sequence of texts

This book does not follow a strictly structuralist guideline as to what should be learnt and in what order by language learners. Language learning is not seen to be linear or additive in the sense that a principled structural ordering of grammar and vocabulary would suggest.

This book is designed as a resource rather than as a course, and it is expected that teachers will select texts according to their students' needs, operating through the thematic and structural indexes for this purpose.

Each lesson is designed to stand alone as an independent unit. The texts are not meant to be cumulative in the way a coursebook is. The language items relevant to each text and lesson are dealt with as they arise in each activity, with no assumptions being made about which texts and lessons have been previously chosen.

However, an underlying premise that guides the sequence of texts though the three sections of the book is that the structures, vocabulary, and syntax become more complex from text 1.1 through to text 3.20. This sequence derives from the writer's experience of what works at what level in the language classroom.

In some cases, quite complex syntax and vocabulary is introduced at the elementary level and this is perhaps untraditional. Because the texts are so small and compact, it is felt that structures that perhaps are not conventionally taught at the elementary level can be introduced through the dictogloss procedure. It is expected that the learners might produce errors in the very attempt to deal with a language point with which they are unfamiliar. They may, for example, produce the incorrect utterance 'I like be here' in the place of 'I like being here'. However, this is the very point of dictogloss – to discover the areas of needs and then teach directly to that need, thereby attempting to address it. We should not as teachers be afraid of error but use it to guide our approach to materials and lesson design.

At times, too, vocabulary not traditionally taught at the elementary level is included in the elementary texts. The point here is that because the texts are so short and because the lexis is to be re-cycled through a number of phases in the lesson (in the warm-up, in the dictation, in the text reconstruction and, finally, during the discussion that accompanies the correction phase), there is little fear that the elementary learner will not cope.

Variations and consolidation

You will inevitably modify and amend the method to suit your own teaching context and conditions. Two ways in which learning can be consolidated are noted briefly below.

Individual reconstruction

During the final stage of the dictogloss procedure, where texts are analysed and corrected, the students are then exposed to the original text. Following this you may re-do the dictation phase (one reading only) with the learners reconstructing the text alone. They may then conduct their own correction from the original text.

Grammatical and textual consolidation

Following the last stage of the dictogloss procedure, the notes may then be exploited by you as a way of consolidating the students' understanding of the structural and textual features of the text studied. For example, the notes can easily be converted to exercises of the following type:

– *Who does 'they' refer to?*
– *Could 'although' be substituted by 'but'?*
– *Why is 'had received' used here rather than 'received'?*
– *If the definite article 'the' is used, would there be any meaning change?*

Authentic material

The texts are nearly all adapted from authentic sources, primarily media sources. Authentic material, generally speaking, is very usable raw data for the creation of dictogloss texts.

Section 1

Pre-intermediate activities

1.1 Marco Polo

TOPIC	**Famous people** **Travelling**
LANGUAGE POINTS	**Past simple tense** **Prepositions:** *from, to, about*
PREPARATION	**1** You may want to bring a map of the world to class. **2** Familiarize yourself with Marco Polo's route in 1271 from Venice to China. (If necessary, see Latham (tr.): *The Travels of Marco Polo*.)

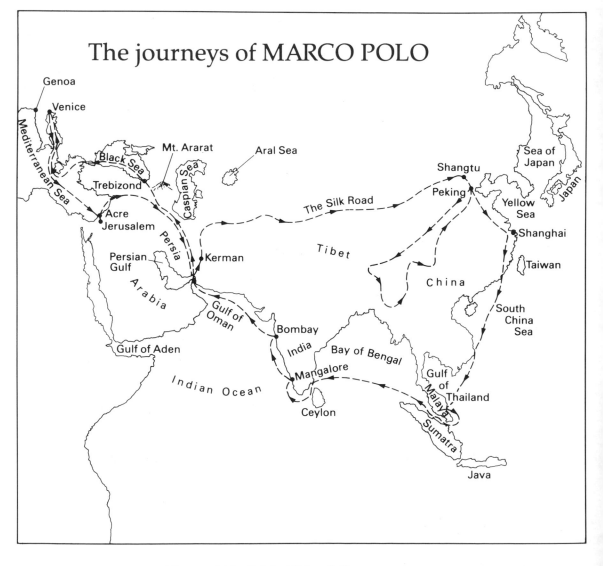

The journeys of MARCO POLO

WARM-UP	**1** Ask around the class to find out what your students know about Marco Polo.
	2 Trace his journey on the world map.
	3 Talk about the journey and get your students to suggest some of the difficulties he might have experienced, particularly at that point in history.
	4 Brainstorm the subject of China.
PRE-TEXT VOCABULARY	**famous** (*adj*) well known **to travel** (*v*) to visit other countries **journey** (*n*) trip **to tell** (*v*) to report, inform
TEXT	**1** Marco Polo was a famous traveller. **2** In 1271 he travelled from his home city of Venice all the way to China and back again. **3** He wrote a book about his journey and it became very famous. **4** Marco Polo was the first person to tell the world about China.
NOTES	**S2** *back* – (Came) back, return. **S3** *it* – This refers to *book*.

1.2 Earthquake

TOPIC	**Natural disasters**
LANGUAGE POINTS	**Past simple tense** **Existential *there*** **Simple sentence structure** **Prepositional phrases**
WARM-UP	**1** Write on the blackboard: *San Francisco – 1989*. Ask your students if any of them remember what happened at that time.
	2 When they have focused on natural disasters, elicit and discuss other natural disasters around the world.
	3 Elicit the students' views on causes. (Discussion may raise theories such as 'the wrath of God', 'nature's way of ensuring population control', and so on.)
PRE-TEXT VOCABULARY	**to search for** (*v*) to look for (someone or something missing) **missing** (*adj*) absent, someone whom people are looking for **rescuer** (*n*) a person who tries to save someone in trouble **suffering** (*n*) pain, unhappiness **destruction** (*n*) damage, ruin

TEXT

1 In 1989 there was an earthquake in San Francisco.   **2** Many hundreds of people died in the disaster.   **3** People searched the city for missing relatives and friends.   **4** Rescuers worked without rest for many days.   **5** There was a great deal of suffering and enormous destruction.

NOTES

S1 *there was* – *There* signals that something happened or existed. It is the existential subject of the sentence whose real subject is *earthquake*. A similar usage occurs in S5.

S2 *the disaster* – The definite article *the* is used here following the first mention (*earthquake*) in S1.

S3 *the city* – The definite article is used, as the identity of the city (San Francisco) is already known.

S4 *worked without rest for many days* – Note the word order: verb + prepositional phrase (of manner) + preposition phrase (of time). The order of the prepositional phrases may be reversed: *for many days without rest*.

1.3 World English

TOPIC

English
Language and communication

LANGUAGE POINTS

Present simple tense
Some and ***others*** as pronouns
Textual reference
Gerunds

PREPARATION

It may be helpful to bring a map of the world to class for this activity.

WARM-UP

1 With the help of your students, identify on the world map the areas with the greatest concentration of English speakers (native and non-native).

2 Ask your students to guess the number of English speakers in the world. 'English' here should include all varieties and dialects of English; 'English speakers' should also include people who speak it as a second or foreign language.

3 When all the students have had a chance to guess, reveal that there are 320 million speakers of English as a first language and 390 million speakers of English as a second language. The student whose guess comes nearest to that figure is the 'winner'.

4 Next, raise the topic of English as an international language. Brainstorm around the class to see what areas of human activity your students think English is used for. If necessary, guide them towards those mentioned in the text (diplomacy, commerce, pop music, aviation, and sport).

PRE-TEXT VOCABULARY

diplomacy (*n*) political relations between governments
commerce (*n*) trade between countries
aviation (*n*) connected to planes and flying

TEXT

1 Millions of people around the world speak English. **2** Some use it as their first language. **3** Others use it as their second or third language. **4** It is the world language for diplomacy, commerce, pop music, aviation, and sport. **5** What's your reason for learning it?

NOTES

S2 *some* – *Some* here works as a pronoun, meaning *some people*.

S2 *it* – This refers to *English*.

S2 *their* – This refers back to *people* in S1.

S3 *others* – This is used as a pronoun, meaning *other people*.

S4 *it* – Again, this refers to *English*.

S4 *world* – This word functions here as an adjective describing *language*.

S5 *learning* – Note the use of the gerund after *reason for*, e.g. *What's your reason for learning/studying/practising/speaking English?*

1.4 I'm Kate

TOPIC

Self-identification

LANGUAGE POINTS

Contractions
Present simple tense
Present perfect simple tense, showing duration (*for*)
Gerund after *like*
Adverbial intensifier (*really*)

PREPARATION

The warm-up section of this activity will only work if you are dealing with a new class, or if your students do not know each other very well. Before the class begins, copy the chart below onto the blackboard or prepare it on slips of paper, one for every two students.

Name	Where...?	How long...?	Age?	Married?	Like English...?

WARM-UP

1 Ask the students to form pairs.

2 Then ask each pair to find out their partners' names, where they come from, how long they have been here, their age, whether they are married, and whether they like studying English.

3 The pairs can either record their responses on their slips of paper, or call out the information for you to put up on the board. This will help them to get the feel of the corporate history of the class.

PRE-TEXT VOCABULARY

single (*adj*) not married
to share (a house with) (*v*) to live with other people

TEXT

1 I'm Kate and I come from Greece.   2 I've been in this country for three years and I really like being here.   3 I'm twenty years old and I'm single.   4 I share a house with two other girls.   5 I am a student and I really like learning English.

NOTES

S1 *I'm* – This is a contraction of *I am*.

S1 *I come from* – Also possible here is *I'm from*.

S2 *I've been* – This is a contraction of *I have been*.

S2 *in this country* – This could also be *here*.

S2 *I really like* – *Really* is an adverb adding intensity to *like*. Note its mid-position between *I* and *like*. An alternative is *I like it very much*.

S2 *like being* – Verbs of liking (such as *like, love, fond of*) and verbs of disliking (such as *dislike, hate, can't stand*) are followed by the gerund form: in S2 *I really like being here*; in S5 *I really like learning English*.

S3 *twenty years old* – This could also be simply *twenty*; or more formally, *twenty years of age*.

1.5 Dear diary

TOPIC

Diaries

LANGUAGE POINTS

Past simple tense
Conjunctions: *and, because, so*
Adverbs of degree: *too* and *very*
Zero article
Contractions
Prepositions: *on* + weekday

PREPARATION

Bring a diary to class.

WARM-UP

1 Display the diary to your students and ask questions like these:
– *What is this?*
– *Who uses a diary?*
– *For what purpose?*
– *What sort of information might be recorded in it?*
– *Have you ever kept a diary?*
– *Would you let anyone else read it?*
– *What would happen (what would you do) if you lost it?*

2 Explain that diaries can be of two kinds: retrospective (to record past events) and prospective (to plan future events).

3 Check with the students to make sure they know the days of the week in English.

PRE-TEXT VOCABULARY

busy (*adj*) having a lot of things to do
difficult (*adj*) hard
movie (*n*) film
tired (*adj*) sleepy, without energy

TEXT

1 I didn't write last week because I was too busy. **2** I started school on Monday and it's very difficult. **3** I met some nice students on the first day. **4** We went to a movie together on Wednesday and we had lunch with our teachers on Friday.
5 School starts again next Monday. **6** I'm tired now so goodnight.

NOTES

S1 *didn't* – This is a contraction of *did not*. See also *it's* (*it is*) in S2 and *I'm* (*I am*) in S6.

S1 *last week* – Note zero article. See also *next Monday* in S5.

S2 *started school* – Note zero article before *school*. This is common with a number of expressions using *school*: e.g. *to school, in school, at school, from school, start school, leave school*. See also *school starts* in S5.

S2 *on Monday* – Note zero article. See also *on Wednesday* in S4.

S4 *our teachers* – *Our* is understood to refer to the English class to which the writer belongs.

S5 *starts* – The present simple tense is used for future meaning in the context of a regular timetable or programme, e.g. *the train leaves at 10 pm, the film starts at 6.30 pm.*

1.6 Garlic, the great healer

TOPIC

Health and medicine

LANGUAGE POINTS

Time expressions
Present perfect simple tense
Past simple tense
Causal connections

PREPARATION

Bring to class a clove of garlic.

WARM-UP

1 In class, ask for a volunteer for a guessing game.

2 Blindfold the volunteer and ask him or her to try and identify the clove of garlic by touch alone. (This stage of the activity should be carried out with the volunteer's back to the class.)

3 If the student is unable to guess, invite others to try, until the garlic has been identified.

4 Then point out to the students that people often have strong attitudes to garlic. Ask your class how they feel about it, and why.

PRE-TEXT VOCABULARY

to use (*v*) to put into action for some purpose
to heal (*v*) to make well again
natural (*adj*) found in nature, not artificial
safe (*adj*) free from risk or danger
antibiotic (*n*) a medicine that kills bacteria
juice (*n*) the liquid part of a plant
infection (*n*) the spread of germs

TEXT

1 All through history people have used garlic for healing.
2 People used it in India and China over 5000 years ago.
3 Because it is a natural medicine, it is a very safe antibiotic.
4 During World War I, for example, doctors used garlic juice because it helped stop infection.

NOTES

S1 *all through* – Or *throughout*. The time phrase has greater emphasis at the beginning of the sentence.

S1 *have used* – The present simple tense is used in combination with *through* to show continuity from past to present.

S1 *for healing* – Note the gerund after *used . . . for*.

S2 *it* – This stands for *garlic*. See also S3 and S4.

S2 *ago* – This word fixes a point in the past. The sense here is that garlic started being used 5000 years ago and has been used continuously since then.

S3 *because* – This is a subordinate clause showing a causal connection to the main clause *it is a very safe antibiotic*. See also S4.

S4 *helped stop* – Note that when *help* does not have an object, the verb that follows takes the infinitive without *to*.

1.7 Child mother

TOPIC

Human interest story

**LANGUAGE
POINTS**

Present perfect simple tense
Past simple tense
***Of* and *'s* genitives**
Adjectives

WARM-UP

1 Ask the students to form groups of about five.

2 Write up a 'word rose' on the blackboard. The words of the 'rose' should be arranged randomly, like this:

child mother   *9-year-old*
                         Brazil
escape   *healthy*

3 Now ask each group to take one word from the rose and develop a section of a short story based on the elements of the word rose.

4 Finally, each group presents their version of the story to the whole class.

5 At the end of the lesson, the students may like to discuss the differences between the various group versions and the 'official' version.

**PRE-TEXT
VOCABULARY**

to give birth (*v*) to have a baby
healthy (adj) well, not sick
youth (*n*) a young man
to run off (*v*) to escape
illiterate (*adj*) unable to read or write, uneducated
remote (*adj*) far away, distant, not easy to get to

TEXT

1 A nine-year-old girl in Brazil has just become the world's youngest mother.   2 She gave birth last week to a healthy baby daughter.   3 The father of the baby, a sixteen-year-old youth, has run off to escape the law.   4 Both parents come from illiterate farming families in a remote part of Brazil.

NOTES

S1 *nine-year-old* – This is an adjectival phrase qualifying the noun *girl*. *Year* does not take a final *s*, as it is an adjective here, not a noun. See also S3: *a sixteen-year-old youth*.

S1 *has just become* – The present perfect simple tense is used here for a recently completed action in the past. The time adverb *just* takes a mid-position between the auxiliary *has* and the verb *become*.

S2 *gave birth* – The past simple tense is used for a completed action at a specific and stated time in the past (*last week*).

S3 *the father of the baby* – Or *the baby's father*.

S3 *has run off* – The present perfect simple tense is used here to describe a recent event in the past where the focus is on what happened rather than the exact time at which it happened.

S3 *the law* – That is, *the police or the authorities.*

Acknowledgement

I learnt about the word rose technique from Mario Rinvolucri.

1.8 A record on wheels

TOPIC

Travel
Breaking records

LANGUAGE POINTS

Infinitives
Negation: *few*

PREPARATION

If you are not an Australian, study a map of Australia, until you are fully confident that you could do a passable outline sketch of the continent on the blackboard.

WARM-UP

1 Draw a rough map of Australia on the blackboard.

2 Ask your students to think of as many ways as possible of travelling across a continent like Australia. Stop if and when anyone suggests roller skates. If the suggestion is not forthcoming, after a while (and a few hints) provide it.

3 Elicit ideas about the sorts of problems a roller skater might face in the course of such a long journey (fatigue, hunger, danger from cars).

4 Alternatively, or additionally, ask your students for ideas on why people go to such trouble to set or break records.

PRE-TEXT VOCABULARY

Asian (*adj*) from Asia
to cross (*v*) to go across
to take (time) (*v*) to last

TEXT

1 Many students from Asian countries go to Australia to study English.   2 They also try to travel around and see as much as they can of the country.   3 Few people, however, manage to travel the way one Japanese university student did.   4 He crossed Australia from west to east on roller skates.   5 The journey took six months and ended in a hero's welcome in Sydney.

NOTES

S1 *to study* – This is the infinitive of purpose providing an answer to the question *why*. We could also use *in order to study* instead of the simple infinitive *to study*.

S2 *the country* – This refers back to *Australia* in S1. Note that the phrase *of the country* does not have to come at the end: it is also possible to say *. . . see as much of the country as they can.*

S3 *few* – This is a negative structure meaning *not many*. It is not to be confused with *a few* meaning *several*.

S3 *did* – This is a substitution for *travelled*.

S4 *on roller skates* – Like many idiomatic expressions, e.g. *on foot, by bike, by car, by plane*, a preposition is followed by zero article before the noun.

1.9 Bullet costs a thumb

TOPIC	Accidents
LANGUAGE POINTS	Past simple tense Interrupted past Genitive *'s*

WARM-UP

1 Explain the context of the activity and give the title. Point out that the word 'cost' in the title can have two different meanings: 'cost' meaning 'what something is worth' in market terms, and 'cost' meaning 'causing serious damage'.

2 Ask the students to guess which meaning is more likely in this text.

PRE-TEXT VOCABULARY

to explode (*v*) burst, break up into pieces
to blow off (*v*) destroy
neighbour (*n*) a person who lives next door or nearby
to bash (*v*) to hit, strike
fence (*n*) a wall or barrier around one's home and property
to rush (*v*) to go very quickly, in a hurry

TEXT

1 An exploding bullet blew off a young boy's thumb yesterday.
2 The boy was playing at a neighbour's home when he found the bullet in the garden.   3 He bashed it on a fence and it exploded.   4 The neighbour heard the boy's cries and called for help.   5 An ambulance rushed the child to hospital.

NOTES

S1 *blew off* – The phrasal verb may be split up by the direct object: *blew a young boy's thumb off*. Note that the verb is in the past simple tense (like all verbs in this text except *was playing* in S2).

S1 *boy's* – Note the genitive *'s* to indicate possession. See also *neighbour's home* (S2) and *boy's cries* (S4).

S2 *the boy* – The article *the* is used here because the reference is definite, having been mentioned earlier, in S1 (*a young boy*).

S2 *was playing . . . found* – This is the interrupted past construction used to show how one (more continuous) activity (*was playing*) is interrupted by another (*found*). The first activity takes the past continuous tense and the interrupting event takes the past simple tense.

S3 *it* – That is, *the bullet.*

S3 *and it exploded* – The conjunction *and* links the two clauses and the sense is one of cause and effect: the bullet exploded because it was bashed on the fence.

S4 *neighbour* – This could refer either to the person who owned the house on the property where the boy was playing (as referred to in S2 as *a neighbour's home*), or a neighbour of that person. The identity is neither clear nor very important here.

S4 *called for help* – Probably, telephoned.

S5 *to hospital* – Note there is zero article in this fixed idiomatic phrase.

1.10 Miracle plunge

TOPIC	**Human interest story** **Accidents** **Domestic violence**
LANGUAGE POINTS	**Simple sentence structure** **Past simple tense** **Articles** **Prepositions and prepositional phrases**
WARM-UP	**1** Tell the class that they are going to hear a story about a 'close shave' in an accident. **2** Explain what a close shave is. **3** Give an example of a close shave, e.g. a slate or tile falls off a roof just in front of some passers-by, but does not hit them; a car skids across a road into oncoming traffic, but miraculously skids back onto the correct side of the road; and so on. **4** Ask the students if they have ever experienced a close shave. List these on the blackboard. **5** If the students seem interested, they may want to discuss whose close shave was the most interesting/horrifying/terrifying/incredible.
PRE-TEXT VOCABULARY	**high-rise** (*adj*) very tall (building) **floor** (*n*), **storey** (*n*) one level of a high-rise building **argument** (*n*) a quarrel or disagreement **to throw** (*v*) to send something through the air **to plunge** (*v*) to fall

passer-by (*n*) a pedestrian
to survive (*v*) to manage to stay alive
bruise (*n*) a painful, discoloured mark on the skin

TEXT

1 A two-year-old girl lived with her mother in a high-rise building. 2 They lived on the fourth floor. 3 One day the father came to visit and an argument started. 4 The father got angry and threw the girl at a window. 5 It broke and the girl plunged towards the ground. 6 At the last moment she fell into the arms of a passer-by. 7 She survived with only a few bruises and doctors called it a miracle.

NOTES

S1 *two-year-old* – Note that there is no final *s* on *year*. The construction (number)+year+old is a fixed adjectival phrase qualifying the noun that follows (in this case *girl*).

S2 *on* – Note that *on* is the correct preposition in this place phrase (not *in* or *at*).

S3 *the father* – That is, *the girl's father*.

S3 *came* – That is, *came to the home*.

S5 *it* – That is, *the window*.

S5 *towards* – This is a preposition indicating motion.

S7 *it* – That is, *the girl's survival*.

1.11 Passive smoking

TOPIC

Health
Environment
Rights

LANGUAGE
POINTS

Present perfect simple tense
Prepositions
Articles

WARM-UP

1 Tell your students that in this activity they will be discussing the subject of smoking. Make it clear to them that whatever their views on smoking, you and they will not be taking a judgemental attitude to smokers as people. This will ensure that in the class 'survey', no individual will feel threatened.

2 Ask the students which of them smoke and which do not.

3 When you have counted them, try to pair a smoker with a non-smoker, or divide the class into mixed groups.

4 Next, ask each group to consider and discuss their own attitudes to smoking in public. This will inevitably raise the question of the rights of smokers versus those of non-smokers, as well as the problem of passive smoking.

PRE-TEXT VOCABULARY

to be aware (*v*) to know about
risk (*n*) danger
passive (*adj*) not active
non-smoker (*n*) a person who does not smoke
to ban (*v*) to prohibit

TEXT

1 For a long time people have known about the dangers of smoking.   **2** Recently they have become aware of the risk of passive smoking.   **3** Passive smokers do not smoke but share their air space with smokers.   **4** As a result Government Departments have banned smoking in the workplace.

NOTES

S1 *have known* – The present perfect tense is used here (and in S2 *have become* and S4 *have banned*) because what is important is the recent actions or events and the fact of the happening rather than the precise time focus.

S3 *but share* – The subject (*passive smokers*, or a pronoun, *they*) is omitted but understood.

S4 *as a result* – This is a discourse connective showing result or consequence.

1.12 Road toll

TOPIC

Accidents
Alcohol

LANGUAGE POINTS

Present perfect simple tense
Passives
Articles: definite and zero
Substitution
Simple sentence construction

WARM-UP

1 Ask the students to think about the factors that contribute to road accidents.

2 Elicit as many as possible (but at least five), and list them on the blackboard. Among their suggestions should be some of the following:

- *poor roads*
- *alcohol abuse*
- *driver fatigue*
- *carelessness*
- *aggression*
- *lack of courtesy*
- *bad weather conditions*
- *sudden illness (heart attacks, bee or wasp stings, etc.)*
- *change in traffic conditions*

3 Then ask the students to rank the factors in order of greatest degree of personal responsibility/seriousness.

4 The students may want to discuss any differences of opinion between them.

PRE-TEXT VOCABULARY	**decade** (*n*) ten years **road toll** (*n*) the number of people killed on the roads in a set period of time **to rise** (*v*) to go up, increase **to injure** (*v*) to hurt **alcohol** (*n*) an intoxicating liquid **drunk driver** (*n*) a driver who is under the influence of alcohol **to endanger** (*v*) to put at risk **passenger** (*n*) someone travelling in a vehicle **pedestrian** (*n*) a person walking on the street
TEXT	**1** Over the last decade the road toll has risen dramatically. **2** Every year more people are injured or killed in road accidents. **3** Alcohol is a major factor in the road toll. **4** Drunk drivers endanger their own lives as well as those of passengers and pedestrians.
NOTES	**S1** *has risen* – The present perfect simple tense is used here to indicate a time focus of recent past continuing into the present. **S2** *injured . . . killed* – The passive is used to give emphasis to the victims, or receivers of the action, rather than its agents. **S3** *alcohol* – Note zero article before this uncountable noun. **S4** *those of* – That is, *the lives of*.

1.13 Baby Hotline

TOPIC	**Parenting**
LANGUAGE POINTS	**Present modals: *can* and *should*** ***Help* + infinitive without *to*** **Gerund after *about***
WARM-UP	**1** Conduct a mini-survey to find out which, if any, of your students have children. **2** If none of them does (or with a very young class), ask them to imagine some of the problems and difficulties of becoming a parent for the first time. **3** Ask them where they would go if they needed information.

4 List some of their responses on the blackboard. These will probably include family, friends, books, neighbours, government services, hotlines, and so on.

5 Using the ideas they have suggested, put up a class survey chart like the one below to show how individuals think they would cope with a new baby. The chart will also indicate what the majority choices of the class would be.

Name	Family	Books	Government	Neighbours

PRE-TEXT VOCABULARY

to dial (*v*) to select the numbers to make a telephone call
to feed (*v*) to give someone food to eat
nutrition (*n*) eating habits
to care for (*v*) to look after

TEXT

1 A new telephone service for parents has started. **2** People can dial the Baby Hotline number to get information about babies.
3 They can find out about feeding, nutrition, safety, health, and sleeping. **4** The service should help new parents learn more about caring for their baby.

NOTES

S1 *has started* – The present perfect simple tense is used to indicate a recent event where the exact time is not as important as the fact that the event happened.

S2 *people can* – Meaning *people are free to/are able to*. Note that there is no *to* before the following verb *can dial*. A similar use occurs in S3 *can find out*.

S2 *to get information* – This is the infinitive of purpose. It provides a reason for the preceding verb *dial*.

S3 *find out* – Note that this phrasal verb has the meaning *get information*.

S3 *about feeding . . . sleeping* – Note the gerund after the preposition *about*. There is another example of this use in S4 *learn . . . about caring*.

S4 *the service* – That is, *the new Baby Hotline telephone service.*

S4 *should help* – The present modal *should* is used here to indicate a strong expectation or possibility.

S4 *help new parents learn* – Note the syntax: verb + direct object + verb. After *help*, the *to* before the next verb (*learn*) may be omitted.

S4 *new parents* – Note the chain of reference through the text: *parents* (S1), *people* (S2), *they* (S3), and *new parents* (S4).

S4 *their* – This refers back to *new parents*.

1.14 Girls step out

TOPIC	Education Sexism
LANGUAGE POINTS	*Will* **for the future** **Present tense after conjunctions of time** **Articles: definite and zero**
PREPARATION	Collect a few examples of sex stereotyping or gender-specific occupations from books, magazines, or newspapers. Also try to find examples of the reverse – instances where job divisions have successfully broken down, e.g. women becoming bus drivers, plumbers, top managers; men becoming nurses, househusbands, secretaries.
WARM-UP	1 Write on the blackboard the question: – *What kinds of work do men and women traditionally/conventionally do?* 2 Next, brainstorm the subject of gender-specific occupations, and list the students' responses on the board. 3 Ask the students in what areas job division is beginning to break down. For example, among the occupations they have named, are there any that are now commonly available to the other sex? 4 Try to extend the discussion by asking for examples from your students' own observation or experience. 5 Elicit their reactions to the changes that are taking place.
PRE-TEXT VOCABULARY	**to encourage** (*v*) to support, give hope **subject** (*n*) a branch or area of study **to choose** (*v*) to pick out, select **broad** (*adj*) wide **career** (*n*) job or profession

TEXT

1 A new plan for schools will encourage girls to study subjects like Mathematics and Science. **2** It will start as soon as the next school term begins. **3** Girls will be able to choose a broader range of school subjects than in the past. **4** The programme will broaden girls' career choices after they leave school.

NOTES

S2 *it* – That is, *the new plan.*

S2 *as soon as . . . begins* – Conjunctions of time, like *as soon as*, are not usually followed by a verb in the future tense. Instead the present tense (*begins*) is used to express a future meaning. See also S4 (*after they leave*).

S3 *broader . . . than* – The comparative adjective (*broader*) is followed by the conjunction *than.*

S3 *than in the past* – That is, *than (they were able to choose) in the past.*

S4 *the programme* – That is, the new plan for girls. Note the lexical chain running through the text: *a new plan for schools* (S1); *it* (S2); *the programme* (S4).

S4 *girls'* – Note the apostrophe after the final *s* to indicate plural possessive.

S4 *career* – This is used here as an adjective qualifying the noun *choices.*

S4 *after . . . leave* – The conjunction of time (*after*) is followed by a present tense (*leave*) to indicate future meaning.

1.15 Book covers

TOPIC

Appearance
People

LANGUAGE POINTS

Pronouns
Modals: *may* and *should*
Present simple tense
Direct and indirect objects

WARM-UP

1 Write the following saying up on the blackboard:

– *You can't judge a book by its cover.*

2 Ask the students what they think the saying means.

3 Next, elicit equivalent proverbs or sayings in their mother tongue(s), and encourage them to think about and discuss the similarities and differences.

4 While they are discussing, write up the following questions on the blackboard:

– *Do you agree or disagree that you can't judge a book by its cover?*
– *Why?*

5 Elicit the students' views and encourage discussion.

**PRE-TEXT
VOCABULARY**

to vary (*v*) to be different
personality (*n*) the features or qualities that make up a person's
    individual character
to tell (*v*) to be able to judge
jolly (*adj*) happy and outgoing
to judge (*v*) to evaluate, form an opinion
appearance (*n*) the way a person looks

TEXT

1 People vary greatly in the way they look and in their
personality.   2 We often think we can tell someone's personality
from the way they look.   3 For example, we may expect a thin
person to be quiet or shy while we may expect a fat person to be
jolly and friendly.   4 We should remember, however, that we
can't judge a book by its cover, and we can't judge a person by their
appearance.

NOTES

S2 *we* – *We* is used to express the idea of people in general.

S2 *tell . . . from* – Note the preposition *from* which links *the way
they look* to the verb *tell*.

S3 *may expect* – The modal *may* denotes a degree of possibility.

S3 *while* – The conjunction emphasizes the contrast (thin versus
fat) signalled by the balanced sentence.

S4 *their appearance* – Note that the plural possessive pronoun *their*
is used to avoid using *his* or *her* in reference to *person*.

1.16 Naturally healthy

TOPIC

Health
Nature

**LANGUAGE
POINTS**

Present simple tense for general statements
Adverbs of frequency
First conditional construction

PREPARATION

Collect some natural herbs and medicinal flowers to bring to class.

WARM-UP

1 Start the session by asking the students what they do when they
feel sick (unwell).

2 Show the class the herbs and flowers you have brought in and
elicit comment, for example, have any of your students ever used
herbal medicines? Do they know anyone who has? What kind of
results were obtained?

3 Discuss with your students different medical customs and
practices throughout the world and throughout history (east versus
west, ancient versus modern times).

pharmacist

PRE-TEXT
VOCABULARY

herb (*n*) a flowering plant used in cooking or medicine
nervous (*adj*) feeling uneasy or worried
tense (*adj*) unrelaxed
to relax (*v*) to rest and feel at ease
camomile (*n*) a flowering plant used as a medicine

TEXT

1 People usually go to the doctor or chemist *pharmacist* when they feel
sick.   2 However, you can often help yourself with natural
medicines and herbs.   3 For example, if you drink warm milk
with honey, you will sleep well.   4 If you feel nervous or tense, a
cup of camomile tea will relax you.   5 For thousands of years,
nature has helped people to help themselves.

NOTES

S1 *usually* – Adverbs of frequency usually take a mid-position
between the subject (*people*) and the verb (*go*). This also applies to
you can often help (see S2).

S2 *however* – This is a sentence connector indicating contrast.

S3 *if you drink . . . you will sleep* – This is the first conditional
construction (*if* followed by *will* in the main clause). Another
example occurs in S4.

S5 *nature* – The word could also have a capital: *Nature*.

S5 *has helped* – The use of the present perfect simple tense allows
for the concept of continuity from past to present.

S5 *to help* – Here the *to* may be omitted.

S5 *themselves* – The reflexive pronoun refers back to *people*.

1.17 The enemy, man

TOPIC

Wildlife
Conservation

LANGUAGE
POINTS

Present tense for general statements and regular activities
Passive voice for process focus
Zero article with plural nouns
Preposition: *for*

PREPARATION

1 Collect a few examples of products of animal origin, e.g. things
made of fur, leather, or ivory.

2 Try to get hold of pictures of seals, elephants, crocodiles, whales,
or any other endangered species.

WARM-UP

1 Show the class the animal products you have brought in.

2 Ask your students to guess what they have in common.

3 Ask the following kinds of questions:

– *Would anyone refuse to buy any of these products on principle?*
– *Why?*
– *What does that tell you about the kind of person he or she is?*

4 Next, display the visuals you have brought in, and ask what products the animals in the pictures are hunted for.

PRE-TEXT VOCABULARY

to club (*v*) to hit with a heavy stick
skin (*n*) the outer covering of an animal or human
to track down (*v*) to hunt or follow the course of (an animal)
to destroy (*v*) to kill
ivory (*n*) the material of elephant tusks
to hunt (*v*) to look for with the intention of killing
oil (*n*) a fatty liquid made from animal fats
species (*n*) a grouping of animals according to their characteristics
to endanger (*v*) to put at risk
fashion (*n*) modern, up-to-date style of clothes

TEXT

1 Man is an enemy to many animals. **2** Baby seals are clubbed to death for their skins. **3** Crocodiles are tracked down and their skins are used for handbags and shoes. **4** Elephants are destroyed for their ivory which is used for jewellery. **5** Whales are hunted for their oil. **6** Whole species are being endangered for fashion!

NOTES

S1 *man* – The use here is generic, meaning *the human race*.

S1 *an enemy* – The article *an* may be omitted here.

S2 *are clubbed* – The present simple tense is used to refer to activities that **regularly** occur. The passive is used to focus attention on the process rather than on the agent. A similar use of the present simple passive occurs in S3 (*tracked down, used*), S4 (*are destroyed, used*), S5 (*are hunted*).

S2 *for* – The preposition here means *for the sake of*. Other examples occur in S4 and S5.

S4 *which* – The relative pronoun stands for the noun *ivory*.

S6 *are being endangered* – The present continuous tense here shows a trend of events occurring in the broad present, that is, a state that began in the past, exists in the present and, as it is not yet resolved, continues into the future.

S6 *for fashion* – For (the sake of) fashion.

1.18 Superstitions and you

TOPIC

Superstitions

LANGUAGE POINTS

Question forms: subject-verb inversion
Gerunds after *about*
Future conditional *would*

WARM-UP

1 At the start of the session, write up a few questions on the blackboard:
– *What does a black cat mean to you?*
– *Or the number 13?*
– *Or throwing salt over your left shoulder?*

2 Ask around the class what superstitions the students can remember. (In a multilingual class you may get a wide variety.)

3 Try to establish with your class which superstitions they think are universal, and which are definitely culture-specific.

4 Encourage your students to discuss their own feelings about superstitions, such as how they feel when they knowingly break a superstition, when they have experienced superstitions being well founded, and so on.

PRE-TEXT VOCABULARY

to have second thoughts (*idm*) to be unsure, hesitate, worry about doing something
ladder (*n*) movable steps used for climbing
to cross your path (*idm*) to meet

TEXT

1 Are you superstitious? **2** Would you have second thoughts about walking under a ladder? **3** How would you feel about a black cat crossing your path? **4** Would you worry about catching a plane on Friday the 13th? **5** Can you honestly say that you have no superstitions?

NOTES

S1 *are you* – Note the reversal of subject and verb in the question form. There are other examples: *would you* (S2, S3) and *can you* (S5).

S2 *would* – There is the sense of an implied (second) conditional construction: *If you had to walk under a ladder would you have second thoughts?*

S2 *about walking* – Note the use of the gerund after *about*. There are other examples: *about crossing* (S3) and *about catching* (S4).

S5 *honestly* – Note the mid-position of the adverb between subject (*you*) and verb (*say*).

S5 *you have no* – Or *you don't have any.*

1.19 Daily print

TOPIC	Newspapers

LANGUAGE POINTS

Present simple tense for general statements
Impersonal *you*
Ellipsis
Present modals: *can* and *may*
Cataphoric (forward-pointing) reference

PREPARATION

Before the class starts, either write up the chart below on the blackboard, or prepare enough copies for one quarter of the class (each group of four students should have one copy).

Name	Newspaper	Number/week	Employment	TV/radio	Entertainment

WARM-UP

1 If you decide to do this part of the activity in groups, divide the class into groups of four and give each group a copy of the survey chart.

2 Each group should carry out a survey among its members to find out who reads a newspaper, how many times a week, and for what purpose. They then report back to you.

3 Collate the results on the board and summarize the overall results.

4 The students may want to discuss significant differences and the possible reasons for them.

PRE-TEXT VOCABULARY

worthless (adj) without value
treasure (*n*) worth a lot of money
to find out (*v*) get information about
forecast (*n*) prediction
real estate (*n*) land and house value
entertainment (*n*) amusement
to wrap up (*v*) to fold paper around
mine (*n*) a source of treasure

TEXT

1 Yesterday's newspaper is worthless but today's is a treasure.
2 You can find out the news in your city or in the world.   3 You can also find out the daily weather forecast.   4 In addition, newspapers offer financial news, employment advertisements, real estate, special features (like food, health, and travel), entertainment, and TV and radio guides.   5 So, while tomorrow you may wrap up your rubbish in it, for today at least your daily newspaper is a mine of information.

NOTES

S1 *yesterday's newspaper* – This is a general reference to any newspaper that is not current.

S1 *today's* – Today's *newspaper* is omitted but understood.

S2 *you* – This is the impersonal use of *you* meaning *people*. (See also S3 and S5.)

S5 *so* – This is a linking word indicating result or consequence.

S5 *while* – This conjunction carries the concessional meaning of *even though*.

S5 *wrap up your rubbish* – This expression is used to indicate the newspaper's worthlessness.

S5 *it* – This refers forward to *your daily newspaper* in the main clause.

1.20 Man in space

TOPIC

Space exploration
Famous people

LANGUAGE POINTS

Clauses in apposition
Past simple tense
Passives
Verb + adjective compounds
Ellipsis

WARM-UP

1 Create the following word rose on the blackboard:

astronaut   *hero*

Yuri Gagarin

space   *Russia*

2 Ask the students to provide comments, associations, responses, or memories, and write up their suggestions at the appropriate point on the word rose.

VARIATION

Another way of doing this warm-up is to divide the class into two groups, those who have heard of Yuri Gagarin, and those who have not. The ones who have not then question the others to get as much information as possible. (This variation will only work if the class is very varied in age and background.)

PRE-TEXT VOCABULARY

flight (*n*) trip
folk (adj) popular among ordinary people
throughout (*prep*) all over, all around
name in honour (*idm*) to give (something) a name in memory of
    (someone)

TEXT

1 It is over twenty-five years since man's first flight into space.
2 This was performed by the Russian, Yuri Gagarin, a farmer's son and father of two. 3 Gagarin became a folk hero not only to his own people but also throughout the world. 4 His life was cut short in a tragic plane crash in 1968. 5 However, his name is kept alive in the many streets and parks that were named in his honour around the world, the world he was the first to see from so far above.

NOTES

S1 *it is . . . since* – This construction: *it is* + time phrase + *since* is a way of measuring the time span between a past event and the present.

S1 *man's* – That is, *belonging to the human race*.

S1 *space* – Note the zero article before *space*.

S2 *was performed* – This past simple passive construction is also used in other places in the text: *was cut short* (S4), *were named* (S5).

S2 *the Russian . . .* – The noun following *Russian* (*man* or *cosmonaut*) is omitted and understood.

S2 *Yuri Gagarin . . .* – This phrase and the one after it (*a farmer's son and father of two*) are in apposition to *the Russian*.

S2 *father* – The *a* before *a farmer's son* also applies to *father*.

S3 *Gagarin* – This proper noun now becomes the key referent to make the rest of the text cohesive: *his life* (S4), *his name* (S5), *his honour* (S5), *he* (S5).

S4 *cut short* – This is a verb + adjective compound. There is another such compound in S5 *kept alive*.

S5 *the world . . . above* – This phrase is in apposition to the previous noun *the world*. It could be expressed (if less dramatically) in a relative clause: *named in his honour around the world that he was the first to see . . . .*

Section 2
Intermediate activities

2.1 The job race

TOPIC	Employment
LANGUAGE POINTS	Articles: definite, indefinite, and zero Simple sentence construction Textual cohesion

WARM-UP

1 Ask the class to think about the stages involved in applying for a job, e.g. reading the advertisements, telephoning or writing for information, writing or filling in an application form, preparing a résumé (CV) and, finally, the interview.

2 Elicit the students' suggestions and write them up on the blackboard.

3 Divide the class into groups of five or six and ask them to rank the stages and tasks in order of difficulty.

4 When the groups have reported back to you, compare the various rankings and discuss any differences of opinion.

PRE-TEXT VOCABULARY

competitive *(adj)* a situation where there are other people wanting what you want and therefore making it more difficult for you to be successful

to seek *(v)* to look for

résumé *(n)* a statement of one's educational and employment history

technique *(n)* a procedure, method, or way of doing something

fee *(n)* charge, cost

worthwhile *(adj)* valuable

investment *(n)* a sum of money spent with the aim of earning money from it in the future

TEXT

1 We live in a time of rising unemployment.   2 This makes the job market very competitive.   3 Many people are now seeking the services of a new type of company to prepare them for a job application.   4 The company helps in a variety of ways, from writing the résumé to training the applicant in interview techniques.   5 The fee is high but many job seekers consider it a worthwhile investment in the competitive race for a job.

NOTES

S1 *we live* – The tense here and throughout the text is the present simple tense used for general statements of the present.

S2 *this* – This refers back to all of S1.

S3 *are now seeking* – The present continuous tense is used here for a time focus that applies to the broad present, or *these days*. The adverb of time *now* takes a mid position between the auxiliary *(are)* and the main verb *(seeking)*.

S4 *the company* – This refers back to S3 where the first mention of the company is made, at which time the indefinite article *(a)* was used.

S4 *from . . . to* – This structure shows the *variety of ways* referred to earlier.

S4 *in* – *The preposition is dependent on the previous training.*

S5 *it* – That is, *the fee.*

S5 *consider it a* – That is, *consider it (to be) a.*

2.2 Intelligence: nature or nurture?

TOPIC

People

LANGUAGE POINTS

Subordinate clause structure
Zero article
Passives
Past tenses

WARM-UP

1 Introduce the subject of heredity by asking your students questions such as:

– *What have you inherited from your parents or family?*
– *What kinds of traits run in your family?*
– *What do you think has more influence, heredity or environment?*
– *In terms of intelligence, which is more important, nature or nurture?*

(Your students are likely to come up with a range of characteristics such as eye colour, hair colour and texture, body shape, height and weight, personality, musical and linguistic talent, shyness, sense of humour, a fiery temper, and many others!)

2 **Note:** in the event of there being any obvious congenital defects among the students, the idea of talking about what they have inherited ought to be abandoned.

PRE-TEXT VOCABULARY

to inherit *(v)* to receive (a family characteristic) through birth
to gather *(v)* to collect
identical *(adj)* exactly the same
to bring up *(v)* to raise (children)
to grow up *(v)* to be raised
remarkable *(adj)* worthy of notice

TEXT

1 Scientific studies suggest that intelligence is at least partly inherited.   2 In other words, intelligent parents are more likely to have intelligent children.   3 Some information about this has been gathered from studies of identical twins who were brought up separately.   4 Although they grew up in different environments, their school results were often remarkably similar.

NOTES

S1 *that* – The relative pronoun *that* begins a noun clause.

S2 *in other words* – This phrase indicates that the previous sentence is going to be echoed in different words.

S3 *about this* – *This* refers to the idea of intelligence being inherited.

S3 *has been gathered* – The present perfect simple tense is used for a recent action where the focus is on the event rather than on the precise time at which it occurred.

S3 *who were* – This is a defining relative clause as the information it contains helps to identify the antecedent (*identical twins*).

S4 *although* – The concessional conjunction introduces a point of contrast between the two ideas in the sentence, i.e. different environment, but similar school results.

S4 *they/their* – These refer to the *identical twins* mentioned in S3.

S4 *grew up* – The simple past tense is used for completed actions/events in the past – other examples of this are *were brought up* (S3) and *were* (S4).

2.3 Freedom of speech

TOPIC	**Politics** **Government**
LANGUAGE POINTS	**First conditional construction** **Passives** **Present modal** *can* **Impersonal** *you*

WARM-UP

1 Tell your students that the topic of this activity is freedom.

2 Next, brainstorm the word 'freedom'.

3 Note the students' ideas on the blackboard.

4 Then elicit the various kinds of freedoms that characterize (and are often taken for granted in) a democratic society, e.g. freedom of speech, of assembly, of political affiliation, of sexual preference, of religious practice, and others.

5 You may find that a number of these more 'political' freedoms have already emerged in the earlier brainstorming. Your students might be surprised to find out just how 'political' they are!

6 Finally, explain the difference between the countable and uncountable uses of the noun 'freedom'.

PRE-TEXT VOCABULARY

feature (*n*) aspect, part, characteristic
to arrest (*v*) to capture (by police)
to dare (*v*) to challenge
to criticize (*v*) to find fault with
informer (*n*) a person who gives information about criminal activity to the police

TEXT

1 Freedom of speech, or the right to say what you think, is the most important feature of a democratic society.
2 Unfortunately, in many countries you can get arrested if you dare criticize the government.   3 In such countries, informers are paid to report on the activities of student groups, workers, and university teachers.   4 If you criticize the government you can get beaten up, imprisoned, or even killed.

NOTES

S1 *or* – The conjunction signals that the following phrase is an expansion of the subject, *freedom of speech*.

S1 *you* – This is the 'general' you, meaning *people in general*. Other examples appear in S2 and S4.

S2 *can get* – The modal *can* here denotes possibility. Another example is in S4 *can get beaten up . . . .*

S2 *arrested* – The passive is used, as the focus is on the process or what happens to the *you* of the sentence, not on the agent(s) of the action. Other examples of the passive occur in S4: *beaten up*, *imprisoned*, and *killed*.

S2 *if* – The conditional introduces the subordinate clause in a first conditional construction. Another example occurs in S4: *if you criticize the government . . . .*

S2 *dare criticize* – Note that where an infinitive follows immediately after *dare*, the *to* of the infinitive may be omitted.

S3 *in such countries* – This phrase links S3 to S2 and provides more detail on the same subject.

S3 *are paid* – The understood agents of the action are the police.

S3 *report on* – The preposition *on* is part of this phrasal verb.

S4 *the government* – This is an on-going reference, first introduced in S2.

S4 *you can get* – This phrase is omitted but understood before the last two verbs: *(you can get) imprisoned or (you can) even (get) killed.*

2.4 Life on the outside

TOPIC

Prisons and prison life
Change and adaptation

LANGUAGE POINTS

Gerund (as subject and complement)
Present participle
Preparatory object construction
Prefixes

WARM-UP

1 Introduce the topic of prison and prison life.

2 Ask the students to consider the case of a prisoner, Joe X, who has just been released after spending twelve years 'inside'.

3 Brainstorm around the class to find out what sorts of skills the students think Joe has learned on the 'inside', and what skills he is going to have to re-learn to cope with life 'on the outside', now that he is a free man.

PRE-TEXT VOCABULARY

to admit (*v*) to state, confess
to conceal (*v*) to hide
stigma (*n*) shame

TEXT

1 Returning to society after having been a prisoner is like going to live in a country with a totally different culture.   2 The ex-prisoner has to re-learn a variety of forgotten skills, such as using money, making choices, and developing relationships with people.   3 Many find it difficult to admit that they need help. 4 Most spend a great deal of energy concealing the stigma of their past.

NOTES

S1 *returning* – The gerund operates as the subject of the sentence.

S1 *going to live* – Here the gerund acts as the complement after *is*.

S1 *after having been* – Or *after one has been*.

S2 *ex-prisoner . . . re-learn* – Note how the morphemes *ex* and *re* function as prefixes to give additional meaning to the word: *ex* = past, no longer, and *re* = do again.

S2 *using . . . making . . . developing* – The gerunds here function in apposition to their antecedent, *forgotten skills*.

S3 *many* – That is, *many ex-prisoners*. Likewise *most* in S4 stands for *most ex-prisoners*.

S3 *find it difficult* – *It* serves as the preparatory object before the 'real' object which is the infinitive *to admit*. This is a common construction when there is an adjective (as here, *difficult*) connected with the object.

S4 *concealing* – Here the *-ing* form is more a participle than a gerund because it functions more like a verb than a noun. Another way of constructing this would be: *most try very hard to conceal*.

2.5 Pre-quake jitters

TOPIC	Natural phenomena Behaviour
LANGUAGE POINTS	Passives Present simple for general statements Word compounds Adverbs Time phrases

WARM-UP

Introduce the subject of premonitions by asking questions such as:

- *Have any of you ever experienced a forewarning that something terrible was about to happen?*
- *How did you feel at the time?*
- *How can we account for these premonitions?*
- *How valid are they as predictors of doom or imminent disaster?*

PRE-TEXT VOCABULARY

to go berserk *(v)* to act in a wild, crazed way
to howl *(v)* to make a long, loud, wailing noise like a dog or wolf
prone *(adj)* liable to, subject to the effect of
zone *(n)* area, region
to affect *(v)* to have a result on
nausea *(n)* a feeling of sickness, wanting to vomit
to release *(v)* to set free, let out

TEXT

1 Shortly before an earthquake animals are known to go berserk: dogs bark and howl, cats run into the streets, and mice run around in circles!   **2** This has often been noted by farmers and other country people in earthquake-prone zones.   **3** Some people, too, are affected with complaints of headache, nausea, and general irritability.   **4** Apparently, before an earthquake, electricity is released by the earth and this accounts for the pre-quake jitters that are experienced by animals and people alike.

NOTES

S1 *are known* – The present simple tense is used here for a thing generally considered truth. It would also be correct to use the present perfect simple tense: *have been known*.

S1 *known* – The passive voice is used here to indicate that the focus is more on the process than the agent. Other examples of the passive are: *noted* (S2), *affected* (S3), *released*, and *experienced* (S4).

S2 *this* – That is, *the fact that animals may go berserk before an earthquake*.

S2 *earthquake-prone* – Note the addition of the adjective *prone* to the noun to create a compound meaning *prone to earthquakes*. This is not uncommon in English, e.g. accident-prone, sickness-prone, failure-prone. Other adjectives can be attached to form a similar compound, e.g. *earthquake-proof* (also *rain-proof, wind-proof, burglar-proof*).

S4 *this* – That is, *the fact that electricity is released by the earth before an earthquake*.

2.6 Battles on the home front

TOPIC

Parent-child relationships
The family
Behaviour

LANGUAGE POINTS

Question forms
Idiomatic expressions
Zero article

WARM-UP

1 Raise the subject of family life, and ask your students to spend a few minutes thinking back over their childhood.

2 Ask questions such as:

– *What sort of child were you?*
– *Were you 'good', 'naughty', or 'somewhere in between'?*

3 Ask the students to decide which of the above three categories they feel they fell into. (It is important that the students should not feel judged in any way about their self-selection into a negative category relating to the past.)

4 Ask the students to work in groups to compare notes about their childhood. Each group should try to reach some consensus about what they mean by 'being a good/naughty/somewhere in between child'.

5 When they are ready, the groups report back to the whole class with their consensus statements. If they wish, they may discuss differences of opinion.

PRE-TEXT VOCABULARY

to drive (someone) crazy *(idm)* to make someone very angry, irritated, or upset
to drive (someone) up the wall *(idm)* as above
to nag *(v)* to ask someone repeatedly to do something
to despair *(v)* to give up hope
at hand *(idm)* available
disobedient *(adj)* not doing what (they are) told to do
harmony *(n)* agreement, good relations

TEXT

1 Is your child driving you crazy? 2 Are you being driven up the wall? 3 Do you nag and nag, day in, day out, all to no avail? 4 Are you exhausted by the battles of everyday family life? 5 If so, don't despair, for help is at hand. 6 A new training programme has started up for parents with disobedient children. 7 It aims to improve parenting skills and increase family harmony.

NOTES

S2 *are you being driven* – The present continuous tense, passive voice is used for an action that refers to a broad present time zone with an understood agent (*your child* in S1).

S3 *all to no avail* – This is a fixed idiomatic expression, meaning *without success*.

S5 *if so* - *So* is a substitution that avoids the repetition of the phrase in the previous sentence: *exhausted by the battles of everyday life*.

S5 *don't* – This is the negative imperative form. The writer is addressing the reader as the understood *you*.

S5 *help is at hand* – Note the zero article before *help* and *hand*.

S6 *started up* – The *up* may be omitted.

S6 *with* – Or *of*.

S7 *it* – That is, *the training programme for parents*, in S6.

S7 *parenting skills* – Note the zero article here, and also before *family harmony* in the same sentence.

S7 *increase* – The *to* before the infinitive verb is omitted but understood to carry over from its use before *improve*.

2.7 One in ten million

TOPIC

Accidents

LANGUAGE POINTS

Past simple tense
***Had better* construction**
Interrupted past time
Non-defining relative clauses

WARM-UP

1 Lead into the topic by talking about tragic accidents, brushes with tragedy, and close shaves.

2 Ask your students whether they have ever experienced anything similar, and how they felt about it.

3 **Note:** we suggest that this topic should not be chosen if there is any known tragedy among the class members.

PRE-TEXT VOCABULARY

out of work (*idm*) unemployed
odd jobs (*n*) unconnected bits of work, usually repair work around a house or building

to chat *(v)* to talk in a friendly way
to wander *(v)* to walk with no definite aim or direction
trigger *(n)* the lever on a gun which is pressed to fire the bullet
to charge (someone with a crime) *(v)* to accuse someone formally
  of an illegal act

TEXT

1 On the last day of the school term, eleven-year-old Timmy stayed home with a cold. **2** It was a rainy day and his mother thought he'd better not go to school. **3** His father, who was out of work, stayed at home too and looked for odd jobs to do. **4** He was getting out his old gun to clean when the telephone rang. **5** While his father was chatting on the phone, Timmy wandered in, picked up the gun, turned it around, pulled the trigger and died instantly. **6** The police did not charge anyone with any crime: it was simply an accident, one of those things, one chance in ten million.

NOTES

S1 *eleven-year-old* – This is an adjectival phrase qualifying the proper noun *Timmy*. *Year* does not take a final *s* as it is an adjective here, not a noun.

S1 *stayed home* – Or *stayed at home*. Note that there is no article before *home*. Likewise, in the next sentence (S2), there is no article in the phrase *to school*.

S2 *he'd better not* – This construction, despite the use of the comparative *better* is not usually a comparison. Here it means: *shouldn't* or *it would be a good idea if he didn't . . . .* It does not have to be negative. *He'd better* means *he should* or *it would be a good idea if he does*.

S3 *who* – The relative pronoun begins a non-defining relative clause. Note the commas which separate the relative clause from the main clause: *his father . . . stayed at home to . . . .*

S3 *looked for odd jobs to do* – Note the syntax here: verb + direct object + infinitive. There is another example of this structure in S4: *he was getting out* (verb) *his old gun* (direct object) *to clean* (infinitive). A common error here is to put another object after the infinitive: *He was getting out his gun to clean it.*

S4 *getting out . . . rang* – This is the interrupted past construction: the first activity (in the past continuous tense: *getting out*) is interrupted by the second activity *(rang)*. There is another example of this structure in S5: *chatting + wandered*. This example is more complicated as there are a number of interrupting actions, all of which are in the past simple tense *(wandered, picked, turned, pulled, died)*.

S6 *it* – *It* functions here as a preparatory subject leading to the real subject *accident*.

S6 *those things* – An expression referring to the things that happen in life that we have little or no power to control.

2.8 Young hero

TOPIC

Accidents
Heroism
Families

LANGUAGE POINTS

Sequence of past tenses
Infinitives of purpose
Interrupted past
Reported/indirect speech

WARM-UP

1 Write the following word rose up on the blackboard:

brother   *screams*   *fire*

young hero

burning   *tap*   *bike*

2 Ask the class to use the word rose to guess the story in the
dictation text.

PRE-TEXT VOCABULARY

to dash (*v*) to run quickly
flames (*n*) fire
to drag (*v*) to pull along the ground
toddler (*n*) a young child
to put out (*v*) to stop the fire
to praise (*v*) to say that you admire someone
to heal (*v*) to recover
burn (*n*) an injury to the skin caused by fire

TEXT

1 A nine-year-old boy dashed through flames to pull his younger
brother to safety.   2 The little boy had been playing with a
cigarette lighter while sitting on his bike.   3 The older boy said he
was standing in the kitchen when he heard his brother screaming
and ran to help him.   4 He dragged the toddler to the bathroom
and turned on the water to put out the fire.   5 Doctors praised the
young hero for his quick thinking and said the boy's burns would
heal with time.

NOTES

S2 *had been playing* – The past perfect tense is used to indicate that
one past action (*playing*) occurred before the other (dashing through
flames to rescue the brother).

S2 *while sitting* – The participial phrase indicates two simultaneous
actions of duration in the past: *playing* and *sitting*.

S3 *said* – What follows here is reported speech. See also S5 for
reported speech after *said*.

S3 *standing . . . heard* – This is the interrupted past time
construction.

S3 *screaming* – The present participle here acts rather like an adjective describing the noun *brother*. Note the fact that coming after (rather than before) the noun, the participle indicates that *screaming* is a temporary rather than a permanent quality or condition of the brother.

S3 *and* – The conjunction here serves as a sequence marker: *and (then) ran to help him.* Another example occurs in S4: *and (then) turned on the water.*

S5 *the young hero . . . his . . . the boy's* – *Young hero* and *his* refer to the older boy, and *the boy's* refers to the younger boy.

S5 *would heal* – *Would* is an example of backshift from *will* in direct speech: *the boy's burns will heal with time.*

S5 *with time* – Or *in time*.

2.9 Safe but sorry

TOPIC	**Accidents** **Human interest story**
LANGUAGE POINTS	**Reduced relative clauses** **Passives** **Past perfect tense** **Articles: definite, indefinite, and zero**
WARM-UP	This is a companion exercise to activity 2.8. Again it involves the class in predicting the gist of the text from the title: *Safe but sorry*, and also from a word rose:

campsite   *searchers*

hikers

helicopter   *safety*

PRE-TEXT VOCABULARY	**hiker** (*n*) country walker **dense** (*adj*) very thick **ordeal** (*n*) a difficult or painful experience **chain-saw** (*n*) a power-driven saw with cutting teeth on an endless chain **landing pad** (*n*) an area of land where a helicopter may land **exhausted** (*adj*) very tired
TEXT	**1** Two hikers, lost in dense forest, spent their second night out in the rain and cold after searchers once again narrowly failed to find them. **2** The two were only a short distance from the place where

their camp-site had been discovered.   **3** The adventurers were finally found in the early hours of the third day of their ordeal.
4 Chain-saws and axes flown in by police helicopter were used to clear a landing pad.   **5** The hikers, relieved and exhausted, were lifted out to safety.

NOTES

S1 *lost in dense forest* – This is a reduced relative clause which, if expanded, would include *(who were) lost* . . . . See also: *flown in by police helicopter* (S4), *relieved and exhausted* (S5).

S1 *after* – The time conjunction helps to fix the sequence of events: the hikers spent the night out + the searchers failed to find them.

S2 *had been discovered* – The past perfect tense is used to clarify the sequence of events. The verb is passive, as the focus is on what was found rather than on who found it. Other instances of the passive are: *were . . . found* (S3), *were used* (S4), and *were lifted* (S5).

S5 *the hikers* – Note the lexical chain that helps to hold the text together: *two hikers* (S1), *the two* (S2), *the adventurers* (S3), *the hikers* (S5).

S5 *relieved and exhausted* – These past participles are part of a reduced relative clause: *who were relieved and exhausted*. They carry the same meaning as adjectives in front of the noun: *the relieved and exhausted hikers*.

S5 *to safety* – Note the zero article in this fixed idiomatic phrase.

2.10 Race for space

TOPIC

The space race
Technology

LANGUAGE POINTS

Passives
Articles: definite, indefinite, and zero
Present perfect simple tense

WARM-UP

1 Introduce the topic of the space race.

2 Ask the class what their views are, for example:

– *How many of you think the money spent on the space race is worth it?*
– *How many think the money could be better spent on earth?*
– *How many are undecided?*

3 Divide the class into small groups (three to five students) and ask them to discuss the following questions:
- *If the money currently spent on space technology were made available to your group, what would be your spending priorities?*
- *What areas would have your attention?*
- *What order of priority would they have? (List the areas and rank them in order of importance to your group.)*

4 When each group has made its decisions, ask the groups to report back to the class to share and compare results.

PRE-TEXT VOCABULARY

to uncover *(v)* to find, discover
to invest *(v)* to spend money on something in the hope of gaining some benefit in the future
to criticize *(v)* to find fault with
to halt *(v)* to stop
to wonder *(v)* to think about
to neglect *(v)* to fail to look after properly

TEXT

1 The planet Earth is only a tiny part of an endless universe where many secrets lie hidden, waiting to be uncovered.   **2** Over the last twenty years, enormous amounts of money have been invested in space exploration.   **3** This policy has been criticized by some sections of society.   **4** Certainly it is impossible to halt the march of progress.   **5** Nevertheless, one sometimes wonders whether our own planet is not being neglected in this mad, blind race for space.

NOTES

S1 *waiting* – The present participle begins this participial phrase that refers back to the noun *secrets*.

S1 *to be uncovered* – *Discovered* could equally be used here.

S3 *this policy* – That is, *of investing money in space* (S2).

S4 *certainly* – Placed at the beginning of the sentence, this marker has great focus.

S5 *nevertheless* – This discourse marker links S5 with the previous sentence signalling a forthcoming contrast.

S5 *one* – Meaning *people in general*.

S5 *whether* – The sense is comparable to *if*. The use of the negative adverb *(not)* increases the doubt being expressed by the speaker/writer.

S5 *our own planet* – This links up with *the planet Earth* (S1).

S5 *is . . . being neglected* – The present continuous (passive) is used to convey an existing and ongoing condition.

S5 *mad, blind* – These adjectives have negative connotations and carry the writer's opinion of the space race.

2.11 Rent strike

TOPIC

Housing and the law

LANGUAGE POINTS

Causative *have* structure (*have* + object + past participle)
Present perfect tenses (simple continuous)
Time conjunctions: *until, as long as, as soon as*
Noun clauses

WARM-UP

1 In the universal struggle to provide a roof over one's head, the battle between the 'haves' (landlords) and the 'have nots' (tenants) often arouses strong feelings and views from both sides.

2 Brainstorm with your students the subject of the rights and obligations of landlords and tenants.

3 Draw a chart on the blackboard, like the one below, and list your students' suggestions (there may be more than five suggestions for each category).

	Landlords	Tenants
Rights	1 2 3 4 5	1 2 3 4 5
Obligations	1 2 3 4 5	1 2 3 4 5

PRE-TEXT VOCABULARY

resident (*n*) a person who lives or resides at a particular place
housing complex (*n*) a place providing independent accommodation for many people
to meet (**a demand**) (*v*) to respond to a request
to carry out (*v*) to do, complete
to claim (*v*) to state as the truth
at risk (*idm*) in danger

TEXT

1 The residents of a housing complex have recently held a rent strike. 2 They have refused to pay their rent until the owner meets their demands. 3 The residents have asked the owner to have repairs carried out. 4 They claim that they have been asking for these repairs to be done for as long as seven years. 5 They claim that their health and safety are at risk. 6 They say that their rent will be paid as soon as their demands are met.

<table>
<tr><td>NOTES</td><td>

S2 *until the owner meets* – The time conjunction *until* is followed by the present simple tense *(meets)* carrying future meaning. There is a similar construction in S6: *as soon as . . . are met.*

S3 *have repairs carried out* – This is an example of the causative *have* construction: *have* + object + past participle.

S4 *they claim that* – *That* begins a noun clause following the verb of saying *(claim)*. Another example occurs in S5.

S4 *have been asking* – The present perfect continuous tense is used to emphasize the durational aspect *(seven years)*.

S6 *they say* – The verb *say* is followed by a noun clause with the relative pronoun *that* omitted but understood.

</td></tr>
</table>

2.12 Chocomania

TOPIC

Food
Behaviour

**LANGUAGE
POINTS**

Neither . . . nor **construction**
Second conditional construction
Impersonal *you*

PREPARATION

See step 4 of *Warm-up*. If you decide to do this, take appropriate action beforehand!

WARM-UP

1 Conduct a class survey to see how much chocolate everyone eats on a daily basis.

2 Identify the chocophiles (those who like chocolate), the chocomaniacs (those who love it), and the chocophobes (those who hate it).

3 Encourage people to talk about their favourite type of chocolate, and when/in what situations they are most likely to have a chocolate snack.

4 You might, perhaps, bring some chocolates to class and share them around!

**PRE-TEXT
VOCABULARY**

random *(adj)* without a definite plan or purpose in the selection of
  subjects
addiction *(n)* a dependence on a drug, e.g. alcohol, nicotine,
  caffeine
to resist *(v)* to say no, refuse a temptation
waistline *(n)* the line around the body at the smallest part of the
  waist
to get away with *(v)* to succeed, manage
fix *(n)* (slang) intake or dose (of a drug)

TEXT

1 If you did a random check among your friends you might discover an amazing thing.   2 The addiction that affects most people is neither alcohol nor nicotine.   3 It's chocolate.   4 Most people can't resist soft, sweet, fresh chocolate and they eat it quite regularly.   5 Apart from the effect on your pocket and your waistline, the habit is neither harmful nor illegal and most chocolate addicts get away happily with at least one 'fix' a day.

NOTES

S1 *if you did* – The second conditional structure takes the past simple tense in the verb of the *if*-clause and the conditional in the verb of the main clause (*might discover*).

S2 *a random check* – Or *a check at random*.

S2 *that affects most people* – This is a defining relative clause providing defining information about *the addiction*.

S2 *affects* – Notice the use of *affect* as a verb meaning *have an influence on* in comparison to *effect* (S5) as a noun meaning *result* or *consequence*.

S2 *neither . . . nor* – This structure is used to link two negative ideas. In this case, the syntax is *neither* + noun (*alcohol*) + *nor* + noun (*nicotine*). In S5, it is *neither* + adjective (*harmful*) + *nor* + adjective (*illegal*).

S3 *it* – This refers back to *the addiction* (S2).

S4 *they eat it* – *They* refers back to *most people* and *it* refers back to *chocolate*.

S5 *the effect* – That is, *the effect of eating chocolate*.

S5 *your pocket . . . your waistline   Your* means *belonging to anyone*. The definite article (the pocket, the waistline) could also be used; *pocket* and *waistline* are used symbolically to refer, respectively, to your financial situation and your figure.

S5 *the habit* – That is, *the habit of eating chocolate*.

S5 *'fix'* – The fact that this is a slang term is indicated by the inverted commas.

S5 *one 'fix' a day* – Or, *one daily 'fix'*.

2.13 Koala suicide

TOPIC

Work stress

LANGUAGE POINTS

Past perfect tenses: simple and continuous
Reported speech
Time adverbs

PREPARATION

1 Try to find a picture of a koala bear from a book, magazine, newspaper, or travel brochure to bring to class.

2 If you cannot find a picture, see if you can borrow a toy koala.

WARM-UP

1 Show the picture or toy to the class, and ask them what they know about koalas and whether they have ever seen one.

2 Write the title of this activity on the blackboard and ask the students to predict the content from the title. There is the risk that your students may go into the dictation thinking that they are going to hear a story about a koala bear who committed suicide. Head off any such expectation!

PRE-TEXT VOCABULARY

zoo-keeper (*n*) a zoo employee who looks after the animals
to take one's job seriously (*idm*) to have a responsible attitude towards one's work
anxious (*adj*) very worried
to hang oneself (*v*) to commit suicide by pulling a rope tight around one's neck

TEXT

1 A zoo-keeper in Japan has killed himself.   2 His wife said that he had always taken his job very seriously.   3 She told police that he had recently been looking after four koalas in the zoo and that this responsibility had made him very anxious.   4 She said he had been worried that the koalas might get sick, as this had happened at other zoos.   5 The police statement said that the man hanged himself from a tree in the zoo.

NOTES

S1 *has killed himself* – The present perfect tense is used as the event is a recent one and the focus is on the fact that it happened rather than the precise time at which it happened.

S2 *had . . . taken* – The past perfect tense is used to denote reported speech. Other examples occur in S3 and S4.

S2 *always* – Note the mid-position of the time adverb between the auxiliary (*had*) and the past participle (*taken*). Note, similarly, the position of *recently* in S3.

S3 *had been looking* – The continuous form of the tense indicates an activity of some duration.

S4 *might get* – The modal *might* is used to indicate possibility.

S4 *as* – As here is used as a causal conjunction.

S5 *hanged* – The past simple tense is used here as there is no ambiguity about the sequence of events.

2.14 Tips for travellers 1: planning a trip

TOPIC

Tourism

LANGUAGE POINTS

First conditional construction
Clause complements after *know*
Present modal *should*
Future continuous tense
Homophones: *weather/whether*
Homonyms
Cataphoric (forward-pointing) reference

WARM-UP

1 Ask the students to imagine that they have won a trip to a country that they have always wanted to visit.

2 Ask them:

– *What will you do before you leave to help prepare you for your trip and to get the most out of your stay?*

3 Divide the class into groups of four or five, and ask them to prepare two lists: one of areas on which they would want information, e.g. food, accommodation, climate, transport, religious, social, and other amenities, and another list of questions they might want to ask, e.g. what kind of food can they expect?

4 If the students feel like extending this section of the activity, members of the groups could, in turn, answer some of the questions and give 'tips' on the imaginary country.

PRE-TEXT VOCABULARY

to find out *(v)* to get information about
to expect *(v)* to predict
to tip *(v)* to give money as thanks
tip *(n)* a piece of useful information
embarrassing *(adj)* awkward, uncomfortable
to miss out *(v)* to fail to do or get something
disappointment *(n)* feeling of unfullfilment
frustrating *(adj)* difficult

TEXT

1 Before they visit a new country tourists should find out as much as they can about the places they are going to be seeing. 2 For example, if they know what weather to expect, they will take suitable clothes. 3 Also, if they know whether to tip or not, they will avoid embarrassing situations. 4 In addition, if they know when the shops are open, they will avoid the disappointment of missing out. 5 These tips should help to make a stay in a foreign country more enjoyable and less frustrating.

NOTES

S1 *they* – This is an example of cataphoric (or forward-pointing) reference, referring forward to *tourists*. An alternative construction is *before visiting a new country*.

S1 *should* – The modal here means *it would be desirable/a good idea.* In S5 (*should help*) the meaning is an expression of near certainty.

S1 *going to* – The *going to* form of the future shows future meaning with a plan or intention existing in the present.

S1 *be seeing* – This is the future continuous tense used to indicate some period of time or duration (that is, the period of the stay in the foreign country). *Going to see* is also correct.

S2 *if they know* – This is the first conditional construction, taking the present tense in the verb of the *if*-clause and the future simple in the verb of the main clause. There are two other examples of this construction in the text, in S3 and S4.

S2 *what weather to expect* – This is the noun complement of the verb *know*. There is a similar example in S3 (*know whether to tip or not*) and S4 (*when the shops are open*).

S3 *also* – This word serves to link S3 to the preceding sentences: *in addition* in S4 serves a similar function.

S3 *whether to tip or not* – Or, *whether they should tip (or not).*

S4 *missing out* – Note that the phrasal verb is in the gerund form following the preposition *of* after *disappointment*.

S5 *help to make* – The *to* in the infinitive (*to make*) may be omitted after *help*.

2.15 Tips for travellers 2: getting around

TOPIC	**Tourists, travel, and cities**
LANGUAGE POINTS	**Generic singular** **Lexical chain** **Present modal *should*** **Infinitive/gerund alternatives**

PREPARATION

1 This is a companion exercise to activity 2.14. For this activity you will need to take to class a transport map of a foreign or unfamiliar city, on which you have secretly set an itinerary from point A to point B.

2 Make enough copies of the map for half the class (if you want the students to work in pairs) or for one copy to each group (if you decide to do the activity in groups).

WARM-UP

1 Divide the class into pairs or small groups (see step 2 in *Preparation* above).

2 Hand out the copies of the map.

3 Ask the students to find the best means of transport from point A to point B.

4 When the pairs or groups have finished, ask them to think about 'sense of direction', for example,

– *How good / bad was your sense of direction?*

5 While the students are reporting back to the whole class, note on the blackboard any particularly successful strategies developed by them for getting around in an unfamiliar city.

PRE-TEXT VOCABULARY

survival *(n)* staying alive
intricate *(adj)* complicated
network *(n)* an interconnecting system
to master *(v)* to understand completely
to get hold of *(v)* to acquire, obtain
local *(adj)* having to do with the particular place where you are
innate *(adj)* natural, inborn

TEXT

1 One of the traveller's greatest problems in a new city is to find his or her way to those things which mean survival: food, a place to stay, and medical help. **2** Most cities have an intricate network of transport and the visitor's first task is to master this transport system. **3** The visitor should get hold of a transport map of the city and become familiar with the local routes and timetables.
4 Armed with this knowledge and an innate sense of direction, a tourist should be able to find the way to any part of the city.

NOTES

S1 *the traveller* – This is the generic singular, where the singular form of the noun is used to stand for the category as a whole. An alternative is to use the indefinite article *(a traveller)* or the plural without an article *(travellers)*. Note the lexical chain operating through the text: *the traveller* (S1); *the visitor* (S2); *the visitor* (S3); *a tourist* (S4).

S1 *to find* – The gerund could also be used: *finding*. There is another example in S2 of an infinitive *(to master)* that could be replaced by the gerund *(mastering)*.

S1 *his or her way* – Traditionally, the male singular pronoun *(he)* stood for male and female; these days, it is preferable to include both pronouns.

S1 *those things which mean . . .* – This is an example of cataphoric reference, pointing forward to *food, a place to stay, and medical help.*

S2 *this transport system* – That is, the one just mentioned: *an intricate network of transport.*

S3 *the city* – That is, *the city where the traveller is at the moment.*

S3 *and become familiar* – The subject *(the visitor)* is understood from the first clause in the sentence *(the visitor should get).*

S4 *armed with* – The past participle *(armed)* begins a reduced relative clause whose referent is *tourist.*

S4 *should be able* – Here the present modal *should* means *there is a good probability.*

2.16 Life in the twenty-first century

TOPIC

Predicting the future
Life and society in the next century

**LANGUAGE
POINTS**

Future simple and continuous tenses
Future perfect tense (past in the future)
Present modal *may*
What's . . . like? construction

WARM-UP

1 Warm students to the topic by eliciting their expectations about life in the next century.

2 The discussion can be further structured by focusing on agreed-upon areas of interest, e.g. leisure, work, medicine, education, marriage, and so on.

3 Extend the discussion by dividing the class into groups, each of which explores one of the topic areas.

4 At the end of the group discussions, each group reports its predictions for life in the future to the rest of the class.

**PRE-TEXT
VOCABULARY**

gadget *(n)* a tool or piece of equipment that performs a particular task
to take over *(v)* to control
chore *(n)* a job around the house, usually boring or unpleasant
leisure *(n)* spare or free time
cure *(n)* a treatment that gets rid of an illness or problem
to colonize *(v)* to start a colony
to relieve *(v)* to lessen or help

TEXT

1 What will life be like in the year 2001?   2 Robots will be doing most factory jobs.   3 Computers will be solving a wide range of problems in business and industry.   4 Electronic gadgets will have taken over most household chores so that people will have far more leisure than they have today.   5 A cure may have been found for cancer and the moon may have been colonized to relieve Earth's overcrowding.   6 Can you imagine what life will be like?

NOTES

S1 *what . . . like* – Note the position of the verb/subject in this interrogative construction: *what* + verb + noun/subject + *like*. There is another example of *what . . . like* in S6 (*What life will be like*). Here the construction is the clause complement to the verb *imagine* and functions rather like an embedded question in that it has a declarative order of elements instead of the subject/verb inversion characteristic of the interrogative.

S2 *will be doing* – The future continuous tense is used here to describe a state in the future which has duration over a period of time. There is a similar usage in S3: *will be solving*.

S4 *will have taken over* – The future perfect tense is used to indicate the completion of an action in the future.

S4 *so that* – This construction shows result or effect. An alternative is to use the present participle: *giving people*.

S5 *may* – The present modal *may* is used to reduce the certainty of the future perfect construction (*will have been found*) to the degree of possibility.

S5 *been found . . . been colonized* – In both verbs the voice is passive as the focus is on the action rather than the agent.

S5 *to relieve* – It sometimes helps to understand the infinitive of purpose by inserting the parts that are omitted but understood: (*in order/so as*) *to relieve*.

2.17 Alpine village

TOPIC	**The environment** **Conservation** **Tradition and progress**
LANGUAGE POINTS	**Phrasal and prepositional verbs** **Imperatives** **Present simple tense for dramatic effect** **Textual cohesion through balanced connectors**
PREPARATION	If you have no personal experience of mountain villages, you may need to do a little homework, looking for pictures of alpine villages and ski resorts.
WARM-UP	**1** On the blackboard, draw a rough sketch of a small, traditional mountain village. **2** Elicit ideas from your students to help you convert your sketch from a village into a modern ski resort. **3** Ask the students to image that they are villagers being asked to vote in a local referendum. (The referendum is being held to decide whether or not to accept a proposal to convert their village into a ski resort.) **4** Ask the students to discuss how they felt about their village while they were in the part of villagers.
PRE-TEXT VOCABULARY	**alpine** (*adj*) having to do with a cold mountainous place **to wipe out** (*v*) to eliminate, destroy **pattern** (*n*) a set of actions or events that are repeated **off the beaten track** (*idm*) not on the main road, hard to find **to come up with** (*v*) to present, put forward **amenities, facilities** (*n*) modern conveniences **to cater for** (*v*) to supply, provide the things that are needed

TEXT

1 Many traditional alpine villages have been totally wiped out to make way for the tourist industry. **2** The process has taken on a familiar pattern. **3** Take, for example, a small mountain village somewhere off the beaten track and virtually unknown to tourists. **4** First, some businessmen come up with the money to develop the site into a ski resort. **5** Then, they put forward plans to build hotels, apartments, boutiques, swimming pools, and other amenities to cater for the tourist industry. **6** Finally, they win across local support with promises of modern facilities, increased employment, and the prestige of progress.

NOTES

S1 *have been* – The present perfect simple tense is used here (and in S2: *has taken on*) to indicate recent events where the focus is on what happened rather than the precise time at which it happened.

S1 *wiped out* – This is a phrasal verb consisting of a verb + adverb particle. The combined meaning of such two-part verbs is usually different from the meaning of their separate parts. Other examples of phrasal verbs in this text are: *take on* (S2), *put forward* (S5), *win across* (S6). Note that *come up with* (S4) is a phrasal-prepositional verb consisting of phrasal verb *(come up)* + preposition *(with)*.

S3 *take* – This is an understood first person plural imperative: *let's take*, meaning, *Let's have a look at this case as an example.*

S4 *first* – This is the first of three textual connectors that serve to give the text its cohesion. The others are *then* (S5) and *finally* (S6).

S4 *come up with* – The present simple tense is used here to give the impression that this event happens quite regularly (as is in fact stated in S2: *the process has taken on a familiar pattern*). The effect of using the present simple tense is also quite dramatic. See also *they put forward* (S5), *they win across* (S6).

S5 *cater for* – This is a prepositional verb consisting of verb *(cater)* + preposition *(for)* + direct object *(the tourist industry)*.

2.18 Moody blues

TOPIC

Human behaviour
Moods and attitudes

LANGUAGE POINTS

First and second conditional construction
Comparatives
Noun clauses
Ellipsis

WARM-UP

1 Choose a topic (say, the Government's performance) and ask around the class what they think of it.

2 As you carry out this verbal survey, list the students' attitudes on the blackboard.

3 Follow this up immediately by asking them how they felt about the same topic the previous week, for example,

- *Have your views on this topic changed in any way since last week?*
- *To what can you attribute the change?*
- *Is it possible to attribute it to a mood swing?*
- *Can you remember any instances where a mood swing has affected your attitude on a 'hot issue'?*

4 Encourage the students to share their experiences if they would like to.

PRE-TEXT VOCABULARY

to miss out on *(v)* to lose an opportunity
stiff *(adj)* severe, harsh
impression *(n)* opinion
converse *(adj)* opposite
spouse *(n)* husband or wife
intuition *(n)* a strong feeling or an understanding gained without conscious knowledge or study
link *(n)* connection, relationship
shift *(n)* change

TEXT

1 Are you likely to miss out on a good job, lose an important sale, or get a stiffer sentence than you might reasonably expect from a judge, if the person forming an impression of you is in a bad mood?   **2** Conversely, would you be less critical of other drivers on the road, more positive about the Government's performance, more tolerant of your spouse, if you had just seen a happy movie? **3** People have always intuitively felt that mood affects judgement and behaviour.   **4** Now new research has supported intuition by scientifically demonstrating that there is a link between shifts in mood and attitude.

NOTES

S1 *lose* – This means *(are you likely to) lose.* See also in S1: *(are you likely to) get a stiffer sentence.*

S1 *stiffer* – The comparative adjective is followed by the conjunction *than.*

S1 *person forming* – This means *the person (who is) forming.*

S2 *more positive* – That is *(would you be) more positive.* See also in S2: *(would you be) more tolerant.*

S3 *felt that* – A noun clause follows *felt.*

S4 *demonstrating that* – A noun clause follows *demonstrating.* An alternative would be to use a noun as object: *demonstrating the link between shifts in mood and attitude.*

2.19 Teachers: an endangered species

TOPIC

The teaching profession
Job satisfaction

LANGUAGE POINTS

Noun clauses
Reported speech
Reduced relative clauses
Second conditional construction

WARM-UP

1 Write up the title of this activity on the blackboard, omitting the word 'Teachers'.

2 Ask the students to try and guess which species is being referred to.

3 Then ask the following:
– *Why should teachers or the teaching profession be endangered?*
– *What is it about teaching that may lead to lack of job satisfaction?*

4 Suggest to your class that at the end of the lesson they might like to discuss with you some of the factors that are mentioned in the text. (It is possible that your students may be quite willing to empathize and to see the teaching-learning situation from the other side!)

PRE-TEXT VOCABULARY

alarming *(adj)* causing worry
poll *(n)* survey
retirement *(n)* the end of one's working life
factor *(n)* one of the things that brings about a result
alienation *(n)* a withdrawal of sympathy
climate *(n)* atmosphere

TEXT

1 Teachers are leaving their profession at an alarming rate.   2 A recent poll showed that the number of teachers with more than twenty years' experience has dropped by half in the last fifteen years.   3 One third of the teachers contacted in the poll said that they would not choose teaching if they had the chance over again.   4 Only sixty per cent of those polled said they planned to teach until retirement.   5 Many interviewed said that factors like stress, isolation, powerlessness, and alienation had contributed to the current climate of dissatisfaction within the profession.

NOTES

S1 *are leaving* – The present continuous tense is used here for the broad sense of the present (these days).

S2 *by half* – Note the zero article in this fixed idiomatic expression.

S3 *contacted* – This is a reduced relative clause. Expanded it would read *teachers (who were) contacted*. See also *those (who were) polled* (S4) and *many (who were) interviewed* (S5).

S3 *said that they* – This noun clause is in reported or indirect speech. See also S4 and S5.

S3 *teaching* – Or *to be teachers.*

S3 *they would not . . . if they had* – This is the second conditional construction using the conditional *(would)* in the main clause and the simple past tense *(had)* in the *if*-clause.

S4 *those* – That is *teachers.*

S4 *until retirement* – Or *until they retired.*

S5 *many* – That is *many (teachers).*

S5 *had contributed* - This is part of a reported speech construction. The past perfect tense is an example of backshift from the present perfect of direct speech *(have contributed).*

2.20 The right to be left

TOPIC	**Left-handedness**

LANGUAGE POINTS

Complex sentences
Subordinate clauses: possessive relative clauses
Articles: definite, indefinite, and zero

WARM-UP

1 As an introduction to the topic, find out if any of your students are left-handed. Ask them, for example:

– *What inconveniences have you suffered as a result of being left-handed?*
– *How could society be more sensitive and more accommodating to left-handed people?*

2 If there are enough left-handers, try to pair left- and right-handers. If not, put the students into groups, each of which has at least one left-hander.

3 The groups should try to find out more by asking the left-handers questions like:

– *What is it like to be left-handed?*
– *What was it like as a child at school?*
– *How have you coped with equipment designed for a right-handed world? (For example, scissors, refrigerator doors, irons, and so on).*
– *To what extent do you feel that attitudes have changed?*

4 Ask the groups to report back to the whole class, and summarize the findings.

5 Finally, ask the students what associations the word 'left' has in their first language.

PRE-TEXT VOCABULARY

generation *(n)* a period of time, about 25-30 years
ignorance *(n)* lack of knowledge
prejudice *(n)* an unfair attitude not based on reason or evidence
butt *(n)* target, victim
to struggle *(v)* to fight
peeler *(n)* a kitchen instrument used to remove the skin of fruit and vegetables

TEXT

1 The fact that we live in a right-handed world is reflected in many languages whose word for 'left' has negative associations.   2 As recently as a generation ago, there was a great deal of ignorance and prejudice about left-handedness.   3 For example, left-handed people were the butt of cruel jokes and, at many schools, left-handed children were forced to write with their right hand. 4 These days, while there is greater understanding, 'lefties' still have to struggle with dozens of daily inconveniences like scissors, cheque-books, door handles, and potato peelers, all of which were created for the right-handed user.

NOTES

S1 *the fact that* – Note the construction *the fact* + *that* + clause. *The fact* allows the following noun clause to operate as the subject of the sentence.

S1 *whose word* – A relative clause follows, introduced by the possessive relative pronoun *whose*.

S2 *as recently as* – This time conjunction links the dependent time phrase with the main clause: *there was . . . left-handedness.*

S3 *right hand* – Even though the subject is plural *(children)*, *hand* remains singular as, logically, each child has only one right hand.

S4 *while* – The conjunction introduces the dependent concessional clause which is further linked to the main clause by *still*.

S4 *greater* – The other part of the comparison *(a generation ago)* is omitted but understood and refers back to S2.

S4 *'lefties'* – The fact that the diminutive is inappropriate to the register of the text is indicated by the inverted commas.

S4 *all of which* – This phrase introduces a relative clause. The multiple antecedents (as indicated by *all*) comprise *scissors, cheque-books, door handles,* and *potato peelers.*

Section 3
Advanced activities

3.1 Locked out by print

TOPIC

Education
Literacy

**LANGUAGE
POINTS**

Reduced relative clauses
Question forms
Prepositional verbs

WARM-UP

1 Ask the students to predict the content of the text from the title.
Keep accepting guesses until a right or near-right guess is offered.

2 Divide the class into groups of four and give each group the task
of compiling a list of ten everyday activities that would present an
illiterate person with difficulty.

3 Put up the lists on the blackboard and discuss similarities and
differences between them.

4 Lead on naturally to a discussion of what causes illiteracy, trying
subtly to incorporate the ideas in the text (especially sentence 6)
into the discussion.

**PRE-TEXT
VOCABULARY**

to cope *(v)* to manage successfully
to disrupt *(v)* to interrupt
to detect *(v)* to find out, discover
to assume *(v)* to take for granted
rate *(n)* speed

TEXT

1 What can you eat if you can't read the menu?   **2** How do you
find what you are looking for in the supermarket?   **3** How do you
cope with street names?   **4** How do you manage to fill out forms at
the bank?   **5** These are some of the problems faced by illiterate
adults in a literate society.   **6** Illiteracy may be the result of any
number of factors: a disrupted early education; undetected
disabilities such as poor hearing or vision; or large classes taught by
teachers who assume that all children learn at the same rate.
7 Locked out of society by the printed word, adult illiterates often
suffer from isolation and depression.

NOTES

S1 *can you eat* – The present simple tense is used here (and in S2 *do
you find*, and S3 *do you cope*) as the time focus is general and deals
with the routine present.

S2 *looking for* – This is a prepositional verb. Other examples in this
text are *cope with* (S3), *fill out* (S4), and *suffer from* (S7).

S5 *faced by* – This is a reduced relative clause: *problems (which are)
faced by*.

S6 *any number* – That is, *there may be more than one factor
involved*.

S6 *taught by* – This is a reduced relative clause: *classes (which are)
taught by*.

S6 *teachers who assume* – *Who* begins a defining relative clause.

S7 *locked out of* – This is a reduced relative clause: *(having been) locked out of.* The understood subject of the reduced clause is the same as that of the main clause *(adult illiterates).*

3.2 Uniformly individual

TOPIC

Human behaviour
School
Clothes

LANGUAGE POINTS

Substitution
Noun clauses
Second conditional
Gerunds
Prefixes

WARM-UP

1 Ask the students to think back to their schooldays, and to recollect some of their experiences. Ask them:

– *How many of you wore uniform?*
– *In your opinion, what are the pros and cons of wearing uniforms?*

2 Try to head the discussion in the direction of the three main claims in the text (see sentences 4, 5, and 6).

PRE-TEXT VOCABULARY

controversial *(adj)* a source of discussion, debate, divided opinion
supporter *(n)* one who supports or backs a particular idea
identification *(n)* a sense of belonging
to outdress *(v)* to use clothes as a means of competition
peer *(adj)* of one's own age group
mode *(n)* fashion, style
de facto *(adj)* in fact, virtual

TEXT

1 The wearing of school uniform is a controversial matter in some countries.   **2** American teenagers don't wear them; nor do the French or the Greeks.   **3** But the British do and apart from a few exceptions, so do the Australians.   **4** Supporters say that a uniform provides a sense of identification with the school community.   **5** They also claim that it removes the competitive tendency young people have to outdress each other and hence divide themselves into 'haves' and 'have nots'.   **6** Another view claims that if uniforms were removed teenagers would end up creating their own 'peer mode' which itself would become a de facto uniform.

S1 *the wearing* – The gerund *wearing* forms the subject of the sentence. The definite article *the* may be omitted before the gerund.

S2 *them* – That is, *uniforms*.

S2 *nor do* – The meaning here is *the French don't wear them either*. Note the inversion of the verb *(do)* and the subject *(the French)*.

S3 *do* – This stands for *wear them*.

S3 *so do* – The meaning here is *the Australians wear them too*. Note the inversion of verb *(do)* and subject *(the Australians)*.

S4 *say that a uniform* – A noun clause follows *say*. Other noun clauses follow verbs of saying in S5 *(they . . . claim that)* and S6 *(another view claims that)*.

S5 *it* – That is, *the uniform*.

S5 *tendency* – Note the relative pronoun omitted but understood after *tendency*: *(that) young people have*.

S5 *outdress* – The prefix *out* indicates the fact of going beyond a certain limit, here in the sense of competing with one's peers. Other examples of this usage are *outbid*, *outmanoeuvre*, and *outlast*.

S6 *if* – This is the second conditional construction with the past subjunctive *(were removed)* in the *if*-clause and the conditional in the main clause *(would end up)*.

S6 *creating* – The gerund follows *end up* with *by (creating)* understood.

S6 *itself* – That is, the *peer mode*. The reflexive pronoun allows an avoidance of the repetition of *peer mode* and also carries an emphatic element.

3.3 The best advice

Growing up
Children and mothers

Reported speech
Embedded questions
Past perfect tense
Substitution

1 Start the session by introducing the subject of advice.

2 Next, ask your students questions such as:

– *Who gave you the best advice when you were growing up?*
– *What sort of advice, if any, did your mother give you?*
– *Did you take her advice to heart?*
– *Now, with hindsight, what are your views on parental advice and on advice in general?*

Note: Some of your students may not know the meaning of the word *hindsight*. Explain to them that it means 'wisdom about an event after it has occurred' *(Oxford Advanced Learner's Dictionary*, 4th edition, 1989).

3 The students' responses should lead naturally into the text.

PRE-TEXT VOCABULARY

wisdom *(n)* knowledge, especially that which comes from the experience of living

to take to heart *(idm)* to accept seriously

appreciation *(n)* gratitude, good opinion

to conform *(v)* to copy what others do

TEXT

1 Tradition says that mothers are full of words of wisdom but how much of their advice is taken to heart? **2** Recently a number of people were asked what advice their mothers had given them. **3** One recalled that her mother had always told her to show her appreciation of other people. **4** Another mother had said that winning didn't matter but trying did. **5** A third had warned her son never to conform blindly to the crowd. **6** People were also asked whether they had followed their mother's advice and most claimed they had.

NOTES

S2 *what advice* – This is the beginning of an embedded question in which the subject/verb order follows the rule for declarative sentences.

S3 *one* – That is, *one of the people who were interviewed.*

S3 *had . . . told her* – The past perfect tense is an example of backshift appropriate to reported speech. Other examples of this are *had said* (S4) and *had warned* (S5).

S4 *winning . . . trying* – These gerunds function as the subject of the noun clause.

S4 *did* – That is, *did matter.*

S6 *whether* – *Whether* is used when there is a choice of two options, in this case: if they did follow the advice or if they did not.

S6 *had* – That is, *had followed the advice.*

3.4 Doctors under stress

TOPIC
Doctors
Health
Society

LANGUAGE
POINTS
Defining relative clauses
Adverb + adjective compounds
Reflexive pronouns for emphasis
Concessional clauses with *while*
Zero article

WARM-UP
1 At this stage, do not give the students the title of the activity.

2 Divide the class into groups of four and ask each group to draw up a list of ten professions or occupations that they consider are stressful.

3 When each group has finished the list, ask the students to rank the ten professions in order of stressfulness.

4 The groups compare their lists and the degree of stress associated with each profession, while you put their findings up on the blackboard.

5 Check to see whether doctors featured in any of the lists, and how stressful their profession is perceived to be by the students.

6 Finally, ask the students what stresses they think a doctor has to face.

PRE-TEXT
VOCABULARY
to encounter (*v*) to meet, face
intrinsic (*adj*) inherent, natural
grossly (*adv*) extremely
to deal with (*v*) to handle, manage
anxious (*adj*) very tense and worried
to realize (*v*) to understand and appreciate
stress-prone (*adj*) likely to suffer from stress

TEXT
1 Each day doctors encounter stresses that are an intrinsic part of medical practice. **2** They work with intensely emotional aspects of life for which their training is grossly inadequate. **3** Interacting with patients who may be frightened or in pain is itself stressful, as is dealing with their relatives who may be very anxious or even deliberately hostile. **4** In addition, doctors often have to deal with the demand for certainty while medical science may not always have clear or easy answers. **5** While many of us realize that stress is a medical problem, few of us realize just how stress-prone doctors themselves are.

NOTES
S1 *stresses that* – The relative pronoun *that* introduces a defining relative clause. There are further examples of this construction in S3: *patients who . . .* and *relatives who*.

S2 *intensely emotional* – Note the adverb + adjective construction. The adverb modifies the adjective, in this case operating as an intensifier. See also *very anxious* and *deliberately hostile* (S3).

S2 *for which* – Placing the preposition at the beginning of the clause avoids ending the sentence with it.

S2 *their* – This refers back to *doctors* in S1.

S3 *interacting . . . dealing* – The gerund serves as subject in both clauses.

S3 *itself* – The reflexive pronoun is used in apposition for emphasis. Note that it has positional mobility: *is itself stressful* (S3), *doctors themselves are* (S5).

S3 *as is* – *As* here has the function of a conjunction and is followed by inverted syntax (the verb *is* + the noun subject, *dealing*). Note that *is* is a substitution for *is stressful*.

S3 *their* – This refers back to *patients* in S3.

S4 *while* – Here *while* means *at a time when*.

S5 *few* – Note that without an article *few* means *nearly none*.

S5 *just* – Here the meaning of *just* is *precisely* or *exactly*.

S5 *how . . . are* – Note the word order in which the subject and verb follow the syntax of a declarative sentence.

S5 *stress-prone* – This noun + adjective compound is quite flexible, e.g. *stress-free, salt-free, accident-prone, illness-prone*.

3.5 Comfort food

TOPIC	**Health** **People**
LANGUAGE POINTS	**Definite article** **Gerunds** **Reduced relative clauses**
WARM-UP	**1** See if the students can guess the gist of the text by predicting it from the title.

2 Next, conduct a whole-class survey on comfort-seeking strategies. Ask the class questions like:

– *What kinds of situations make you feel bad?*
– *Do you feel you need comfort when you feel bad?*
– *How do you respond to your need for comfort?*
– *Are you attracted to or repelled by food at such times?*
– *If you are attracted, what do you do about it?*
– *What do you eat, where, and with whom? (by yourself or in company?)*

3 Finally, steer the discussion towards the ideas in sentences 3, 4, and 5 of the text.

4 Note: it is suggested that the whole matter be treated tactfully, especially if it is felt it might be a touchy subject for some (overweight) students.

PRE-TEXT VOCABULARY

temptation (*n*) something which attracts you to it, usually unwisely
soothing (*adj*) calming, comforting
to remind (*v*) to make you remember
distraction (*n*) something which takes your attention from something else
tactile (*adj*) related to touch
starchy (*adj*) food containing starch, like potatoes
to trigger (*v*) to start off, bring about
serotonin (*n*) the name of a chemical in the brain

TEXT

1 An important relationship exists between food and comfort.
2 In times of stress, when one is depressed, anxious or hurt, the temptation may be to turn to food – soft, smooth, sweet, soothing food.   3 Many people turn to the food that reminds them of their childhood, of being loved and cared for.   4 Others find as much comfort in the distraction offered by the act of preparing food – the smells, tactile sensations, and physical work of the kitchen.
5 Scientists researching the link between foods and moods believe that certain sweet and starchy foods trigger an increase in the chemical called serotonin in the brain, making us sleepy and less sensitive to pain.   6 The problem with using food as a source of comfort is that it may lead to overeating and overweight.

NOTES

S2 *the temptation* – Or *one may be tempted to*.

S2 *soft, smooth* – This phrase is in apposition to *food*. A similar construction is found in S4, again in apposition to *food*. In each case a dash separates the antecedent from the amplifying phrase.

S3 *the food* – The definite article *the* is used as *food* is made definite by the defining relative clause that follows (= post-modification). There are other examples of post-modification in this text: in S4 (*the distraction, the act, the smells*), S5 (*the link, the chemical*).

S3 *the food that* – *That* begins a defining relative clause which provides essential information about *food*.

S3 *of being loved* – The gerund here is the indirect object of *remind*.

S4 *others* – This balances *many people* in S3.

S4 *offered* – That is, (*which is*) *offered*.

S4 *preparing food* – The gerund here is the agent of the passive verb *offered*.

S5 *scientists researching* – That is, *scientists (who are) researching*.

S5 *making* – The participle clause has an adverbial function adding meaning to the finite verb *trigger*.

S6 *overeating* – The gerund here is the object of the verb *lead to*.

3.6 Phobia poll

TOPIC

Human behaviour and attitudes
Fear
Male and female differences

LANGUAGE POINTS

Noun clauses
Comparative constructions
Gerunds

WARM-UP

1 Give everyone in the class a small slip of paper. Ask everyone (including yourself) to write down the thing that most frightens them.

2 Collect the pieces of paper and read them out one by one, each time eliciting comment and reaction from the class. The person whose fear is being discussed may or may not want to own up. Your students should be aware that this is acceptable. (An alternative might be to brainstorm 'fears' onto one half of the blackboard. Stop when there are about ten on the board. Then divide the class into groups of about four. Each group should rank the fears on a continuum from the least fearsome to the most fearsome. End by comparing the various results.)

3 Lead on to a more general discussion. Try to include lexis from sentence 2 of the text. (Note that the fears mentioned are not linguistically uniform.) Also try to steer the discussion towards issues that are covered in the text, e.g. differences between men and women, the correlation between fear and age, and between fear and educational level.

4 Finally, give the class the title of the text and clarify any questions concerning it.

PRE-TEXT VOCABULARY

inherently (*adv*) by nature
to be inclined (*v*) to be willing
to jump to a conclusion (*idm*) to make a hasty deduction
to own up (*v*) to admit

TEXT

1 A recent poll on the subject of fear asked people to respond to a list of eight common phobias. 2 The list included speed, heights, lifts, crowds, flying, confined spaces, open spaces, and the dark. 3 It excluded things like snakes and spiders that are inherently dangerous. 4 The poll revealed that many more women than men admitted to experiencing fear. 5 Before you immediately jump to the conclusion that men are braver than women, you should be warned that one explanation for the figures may be that men are less inclined than women to owning up to fear. 6 The poll also indicated that fear tends to increase with age and decrease with educational level.

NOTES

S3 *it* – That is, *the list*.

S3 *that are inherently dangerous* – This is a defining relative clause, as the information in it is needed to give the subject a clear meaning.

S4 *revealed that* – Reported speech follows *revealed* in a noun clause.

S4 *more women than men* – Note that the latter part of the comparison (*than men*) can come at the end of the sentence: *more women admitted to experiencing fear than men*. There is a similar construction in S5 where once again, the latter part of the comparative may be moved: *men are less inclined to owning up to fear than women*.

S4 *experiencing* – Note the gerund after the preposition *to* following *admitted*.

S5 *you* – Meaning the reader.

S5 *warned that* – Reported speech follows *warned* in a noun clause.

S5 *the figures* – That is, as implied in S4.

S5 *owning up* – The gerund follows *to* after *inclined*.

S6 *indicated that* – Reported speech follows *indicated* in a noun clause.

S6 *and decrease* – Note what is omitted but understood: *and (fear tends to) decrease*.

3.7 Jungle boy

TOPIC

Behaviour

LANGUAGE POINTS

Present participles
Passives
Perfect infinitive
Reduced clauses
Non-defining relative clauses

WARM-UP

1 Probably most of your students will have heard of Tarzan. Elicit from them what they know about him.

2 Ask them to think about what a human being would be like if he or she were raised by animals in the jungle.

3 Next ask:

– *What do you see as the main differences between animals and humans, and between life in the jungle and in so-called civilization?*

PRE-TEXT VOCABULARY

orphanage (*n*) an institution for children whose parents are dead
to lose one's parents (*v*) to lose through death
to mother (*v*) to look after, care for, like a mother
to get about (*v*) to move from place to place

to clench (*v*) to close tightly
still (*adj*) without moving
to squat (*v*) to sit in a crouching position
rump (*n*) the back part, bottom of an animal
indiscriminately (*adv*) without caring to choose
to shun (*v*) to avoid

TEXT

1 A child with all the behaviour of a monkey has been found in Africa.   2 He was found living with a tribe of monkeys and taken to an orphanage.   3 The boy, whose age is estimated to be between five and seven, is believed to have lost his parents at about the age of one and to have been mothered by a chimpanzee or a gorilla.   4 The jungle boy gets about by jumping like a monkey with his hands clenched; when still, he squats on his rump, and if approached, scratches.   5 He grunts and squeals and eats indiscriminately – grass, clothes, bedding, even stones.
6 Shunning the company of humans, he neither smiles nor shows any interest whatever in his surroundings.

NOTES

S2 *living* – The participial clause here functions as an object complement after the verb *found*.

S2 *and* – The conjunction here links the two clauses and indicates a sequence of events.

S3 *to have lost* – This is the perfect infinitive used for an event in the past. Another example, this time in the passive occurs later in S3: *to have been mothered*.

S4 *clenched* – The past participle placed after the noun functions here rather like an adjective describing the noun *hands*.

S4 *when still* – That is, *when (he is) still*.

S4 *scratches* – The subject *he* is understood and does not need repeating.

S6 *shunning* – This participial phrase can be used in this way as it shares a common subject with the main clause of the sentence, that is *he*.

S6 *whatever* – This serves to intensify the negative. Another way of expressing the same idea is: *any interest at all*.

3.8 Whose aid?

TOPIC

International politics
Economics

LANGUAGE POINTS

Present modals: *may* and *can*
Connectors of cause and result
Review of prepositions
Textual cohesion through progressive connectors

WARM-UP

1 Write the following word rose up on the blackboard:

foreign adviser   *local population*

developing country

aid   *conflict*

2 Tell the students that for this activity, they are not required to guess a story from the word rose. They are to do a free association from the words.

3 Add their suggestions at the appropriate point on the rose.

4 Finally, discuss the issue of foreign aid, gently steering the discussion to cover the topic areas dealt with in the text.

PRE-TEXT VOCABULARY

undue *(adj)* improper, more than is right
to be aware of *(v)* to know about, realize
host *(n)* one who receives visitors
to overlook *(v)* to fail to pay attention
to trample *(v)* to walk over, pay no respect to
to hold up *(v)* to delay
livelihood *(n)* a means of earning a living

TEXT

1 The whole question of aid to developing countries raises a number of issues.   **2** Firstly, the presence of foreign advisers in a third world country has political implications, as these external experts may have an undue influence over local politicians.
3 Furthermore, outsiders are unlikely to be aware of the host country's customs and traditions, with the result that aid projects could overlook or even trample on sensitive local matters.   **4** This may lead to conflict which, at the very least, may hold up progress and at the worst, may stir up hostility and aggression.   **5** Finally, new aid schemes such as dams and mining can have undesirable effects on the environment as well as on local livelihoods.

NOTES

S1 *raises* – The singular subject of the verb is *question*.

S2 *as* – This is a causal connector linking the main clause to the subordinate one; *because* or *since* could also be used here.

S2 *these external experts* – That is, *the foreign advisers* mentioned earlier in the same sentence.

S2 *over* – Or *on*.

S3 *with the result that* – Or *resulting in*. Either phrase shows consequence or result.

S3 *on* – Or *over*.

S4 *at the very least* – This phrase balances the later one, *at the worst*.

S5 *effect* – Note the preposition *on* that links this noun with the following prepositional phrases (*on the environment . . . on local livelihoods*).

3.9 Jet lag

TOPIC

Jet lag
Travel
The body

LANGUAGE POINTS

Complex sentences
Subordinate clauses
Reduced relative clauses

WARM-UP

1 Initiate the topic and the discussion by relating a personal experience of jet lag as follows: *One day when I was travelling from . . . to . . .*, etc. Describe your symptoms at the time, and the ways in which you dealt with them.

2 By telling the students of your experiences you may remind them of similar experiences they have had and so 'loosen tongues'.

3 Now ask:

– *Has any of you had personal experience of jet lag?*
– *What happened and how did you feel?*
– *How long did it take you to recover?*
– *What strategies did you use to make yourself feel better?*

4 Next, paraphrase the gist of the text by explaining the mechanics of jet lag. Try to incorporate the key concepts and lexis of the text into your explanation (jet lag involves the body's internal clock, external cues, time shifts, and disorientation).

PRE-TEXT VOCABULARY

to regulate *(v)* to control
signals *(n)* signs
zone *(n)* a special area
cue *(n)* signal
numb *(adj)* without feeling
to synchronize *(v)* to plan the timing of one thing so that it matches another

TEXT

1 Our lives are regulated by many cycles, some external, like day, night, and seasons, and some internal, like the bodily signals that tell us when to sleep, eat, be active, alert, and so forth. 2 When we travel long distances east or west, we are rapidly transported into a different time zone. 3 The external cues have changed and we discover, for example, that the sun is rising when we expect to be asleep. 4 The body becomes confused at the time shift and responds by attempting to re-set the internal clock to correspond with the new time zone. 5 The result is 'jet lag', a condition characterized by a numbing mental and physical exhaustion and disorientation. 6 Jet lag is a term used to describe what happens when the body's internal clock is no longer synchronized with the external environment.

NOTES

S1 *some external* – That is, *some (are) external*. See also *some (are) internal*.

S1 *the bodily signals that* – The relative clause *that* begins a defining relative clause.

S3 *have changed* – The present simple tense *(change)* could be used here.

S4 *the body* – Or *our bodies* or *our body*.

S4 *confused at* – *By* could be used instead of *at*.

S4 *to correspond* – Or *so that it corresponds*.

S5 *a condition* – This clause is in apposition with *jet lag*.

S5 *characterized* – This is a reduced relative clause which if expanded would read *a condition (which is) characterized*. See also in S6, *a term (which is) used*.

S6 *synchronized* – The past participle might be considered part of the passive construction: *is . . . synchronized* or may be considered an adjective after the verb *to be (is)*.

S6 *what happens when* – This clause is the complement of the verb *describe*.

3.10 Leisure stress

TOPIC

Leisure and work
Behaviour

LANGUAGE POINTS

Reduced relative clauses
Defining relative clauses
Clauses in apposition

WARM-UP

1 Ask your students to form pairs with the person on their right. Each pair should find out from each other how they spend their leisure time.

2 When all the pairs have finished, regroup the class into three large groups consisting respectively of workaholics, leisure-holics, and those who see themselves as well balanced!

3 Ask the newly formed groups to share their attitudes to leisure.

4 Finally, introduce the notion of 'leisure stress' and invite interpretations from the class.

PRE-TEXT VOCABULARY

to take a break *(idm)* to have a rest from work
prone *(adj)* likely to experience
schedule *(n)* timetable, work programme
pace *(n)* speed at which an activity is performed
to cope *(v)* to deal with, manage
tedium *(n)* monotony, boredom
vicious *(adj)* nasty, cruel
to unwind *(v)* to relax, enjoy a break from work

| TEXT | 1 A phenomenon that has recently been identified in western societies is leisure stress, an anxiety experienced by people who hate taking a break. 2 Certain personality types are particularly prone to this problem, people who are high-achievers, competitive by nature, and success-motivated. 3 Energized by a hectic work pace and a busy schedule, such people are unable to cope with unstructured spare time. 4 For them leisure and relaxation equate with tedium and boredom. 5 In some cases people who have poorly developed social skills begin to avoid situations which require them to interact informally. 6 A vicious circle develops and so they never acquire the skills that would help them unwind. |

NOTES

S1 *phenomenon that* – This is a defining relative clause.

S1 *an anxiety* – This clause is in apposition to *leisure stress*.

S1 *experienced* – This is part of a reduced relative clause which if expanded would read *(which is) experienced*.

S2 *problem* – This could be followed by a dash or a colon.

S2 *people who* – This is a defining relative clause which here works in apposition to *certain personality types*. Other defining relative clauses are to be found in S5: *people who* and *situations which*, and S6: *the skills that*.

S2 *success-motivated* – This is a reduced relative clause transformed into a compound adjective made up of noun + past participle. The original clause would have been: *people who are motivated by success*.

S3 *energized* – This reduced relative clause works rather like an adjectival construction. It can operate like this because its implied subject is the same as the subject of the main clause *(such people)*.

S4 *them* – That is, *such people* (S3). See also *they, them* (S6).

S5 *begin to avoid* – Or, *begin avoiding*.

S6 *unwind* – After *help*, the *to* of the infinitive is omitted: *help them (to) unwind*.

3.11 Conserving family history

TOPIC

History
Families
Identity

LANGUAGE POINTS

Zero article
Sentence connectors

WARM-UP

1 As this activity involves a longish visualization, it is important that the students feel thoroughly relaxed. If you feel they need a little help, suggest that they sit back in their chairs, shut their eyes, drop their shoulders, and take a few slow, deep breaths.

2 Next, tell them the following:

– *Imagine that you are going home one day, and as you approach your house, you smell smoke. You very soon realize that it is your home on fire. Fortunately, you soon find out that all the members of your family and household, including your pets, are safe and unhurt. As you are standing there, feeling very relieved, a fireman on a ladder calls out to let you know that he can save one thing for you from your house. You think for a moment and then tell him what you want to save.*

3 Now gently ask the students to open their eyes and move around the class sharing their responses to the situation with the other students.

4 Then ask them to relate their responses to you, and collate them on the blackboard.

5 With the help of the students, try to categorize the responses.

6 Finally, raise the subject of family memorabilia and elicit views on their relative importance to your class.

Acknowledgement

The idea for this warm-up is inspired by Moskowitz: *Caring and Sharing in the Foreign Language Classroom.*

PRE-TEXT VOCABULARY

to sever *(v)* to cut, break off a connection
ancestral *(adj)* relating to one's ancestors
corporate *(adj)* relating to corporations or large companies
to set (someone) adrift *(v)* to send (someone) away without friends, family, or livelihood
anchorage *(n)* safe connection, link
memorabilia *(n)* a collection of personal mementoes
to calculate *(v)* to estimate
to assure *(v)* to give confidence, comfort
to urge *(v)* to advise, recommend highly

TEXT

1 Today, more than at any other time in history, vast numbers of people are being forced to sever their ancestral ties. **2** Emigration, wars, corporate mobility, and family breakdown have set thousands adrift, leaving them without any anchorage to their past except for their precious family mementoes: records, photos, letters, books, paintings, diaries. **3** Such memorabilia are incalculably precious as they serve to assure people that they belong somewhere. **4** Yet this assurance is always at risk not only from natural disasters like fire and flood but also from the natural daily process of physical deterioration. **5** As a result, some family historians are urging people to learn the basic techniques of conservation so as to preserve their family records for future generations.

NOTES

S1 *are being forced* – The present continuous tense is used for an action in the broad present (with a 'nowadays' meaning). Note the passive voice as the *people* are the receivers of the action, the agent of which is detailed in S2: *emigration, wars, corporate mobility, and family breakdown.*

S2 *have all set* – The *all* reflects the compound subject.

S2 *set . . . adrift* – Note that this phrasal verb requires its direct object to be positioned between the verb and the preposition.

S2 *leaving* – The present participle could be replaced by another finite clause linked with *and*: *and left them.* In this case, with two finite verbs linked by the conjunction *and*, a time sequence would be implied.

S3 *such memorabilia* – That is, all the mementoes (*records, photos,* and so on) listed in S2.

S4 *yet* – The connector indicates a forthcoming contrast.

S4 *not only . . . but also* – Note the balance created in the sentence by this construction.

S5 *as a result* – The connector indicates that a statement of consequence is forthcoming.

S5 *are urging* – This is the same usage commented on in S1 (*are being forced*), the broad present for a 'nowadays' meaning.

3.12 Women's intuition

TOPIC	**Women** **Behaviour**
LANGUAGE POINTS	**Causal connections** **Defining relative clauses** **Articles: definite, indefinite, and zero** **Adverbs**
WARM-UP	**1** Ask your students to name the five senses (touch, taste, sight, hearing, smell).

2 List them on the blackboard, and number them as the students call them out.

3 Next add the number 6 under the five senses and ask what your students think it represents. Ask them:

– *What do you know about the sixth sense?*

Make sure that in the ensuing discussion the word 'intuition' is incorporated.

4 Tell the class that there is a certain kind of intuition known as feminine or women's intuition. Find out to what extent your class believe in this.

5 As the discussion progresses, try to bring in consideration of causes (sentence 2 of the text) and results (sentences 3, 4, and 5).

PRE-TEXT VOCABULARY

perceptive *(adj)* quick to understand
to bring up *(v)* to raise (children)
channel *(n)* a way or medium of communicating
to pick up *(v)* to recognize
to decipher *(v)* to interpret meaning
to get away with *(v)* to escape punishment
conversely *(adv)* in the opposite way
to pull the wool over someone's eyes *(idm)* to deceive someone
negotiator *(n)* a person who works out agreements through discussion

TEXT

1 The fact that women generally are more perceptive than men has given rise to what is commonly known as 'women's intuition'.
2 This quality is particularly evident in women who have brought up young children, for a mother who has a young child relies largely on non-verbal channels of communication.   3 Thus, many women develop an ability to pick up and decipher non-verbal signals, as well as an accurate eye for small detail.   4 This is why few husbands can lie to their wives and get away with it and why, conversely, many women can pull the wool over a man's eyes without his realizing it.   5 It is also believed to be the reason why women often become more perceptive and skilled negotiators than men.

NOTES

S1 *the fact that* – The structure *the fact* + *that* allows the *that* clause to serve as the subject of the sentence.

S1 *what is commonly known as* – This is a nominal relative clause. *What* acts as both a noun and a relative pronoun together (*the thing that*).

S2 *this quality* – That is, as stated in S1.

S2 *women who* – A defining relative clause follows, as the information in it is necessary and not additional. See also, in the same sentence *a mother who has a young child*.

S2 *for* – This is a causal connector showing reason to account for *women's intuition*.

S4 *this is why* – Understood but omitted here is *the reason*: *this is the reason why*. *Why* operates as a relative pronoun (meaning *for which*) after the noun *reason*. Note that it is not the interrogative use of *why* and hence the subject-verb order follows the pattern for declarative sentences. There is another example of this in the same sentence: *and why, conversely*. In S5 the structure is used again, this time with *reason* included: *the reason why women*.

S4 *his realizing* – Note the use of the possessive pronoun before the gerund. In more informal English *him* would be more appropriate than *his*.

S5 *it* – That is, *women's intuition*.

3.13 Middle children

TOPIC

The family
Behaviour
Society

**LANGUAGE
POINTS**

Present participial clauses: stative and dynamic verbs
Generics
Compounds

WARM-UP

1 Create four areas in the classroom (such as the four corners).

2 Put up a label in each of the areas:

First born   *Only child*

Last born   *Middle child*

3 Now ask your students to go to the area of the room they belong to according to their birth order.

4 Once the groups have formed in their respective areas, ask them to share their experiences of being an only child/last born/first born/middle child. (If there happens to be an area with only one student, you might like to pair up with him or her or send the student to another group as an observer.)

5 Ask the students to reassemble as a class, and focus on the position of middle children. Find out from the middle children in the class:

– *Do your experiences have anything in common?*
– *Can you make any generalizations about middle children from this?*

6 Finally, reveal the title of the text.

**PRE-TEXT
VOCABULARY**

to neglect *(v)* to pay little attention to, to fail to look after
sibling *(n)* a brother or sister
flexible *(adj)* to change or adapt easily
high-achiever *(n)* someone who aims for success
peer *(n)* someone of one's own age or rank
to orient *(v)* to aim or direct one's attention towards
merit *(n)* benefit, advantage
to mediate *(v)* to try to resolve a disagreement

TEXT

1 Middle children, being neither the oldest nor the youngest in the family, tend to feel neglected and insecure.   2 Yet, being sandwiched between siblings, they are often the family peace-makers, and so they learn to be flexible and realistic.   3 Research has shown that while first-borns tend to be high-achievers, second-borns tend to be more peer-oriented, having more friends and socializing more easily.   4 These days, with more people choosing small families, the middle child is disappearing.   5 Opinion is divided on the merits of this, with some psychologists predicting healthier adults and others fearing the loss of the middle child's mediating influence.

NOTES

S1 *being* – The present participle of the stative verb *be* suggests the idea of reason or cause: *middle children, because they.* A similar usage occurs in S2, *being sandwiched.*

S2 *the family peace-makers* – The definite article + plural noun is here used to express the generic. Compare the plural noun with zero article *(middle children)* in S1, and definite article + singular noun *(the middle child)*, which are alternative ways of expressing the generic.

S2 *peace-makers* – This is a compound noun consisting of noun + verb, with the verb *make* turned into a noun *(maker)* by the addition of the suffix *-er*. This is a common construction in English. Other examples are *breadwinner* and *lawmaker*. A similar process occurs in *high-achiever* (S3), this time composed of adjective + verb.

S3 *while* – A concessional clause, implying a forthcoming contrast.

S3 *first-borns* – The adjective is used as a noun, with *children* understood. See also *second-borns* (S3). In both cases, the noun is a compound, composed of adjective + past participle.

S3 *peer-oriented* – Another compound, this time adjectival in function, composed of noun + past participle. In fact this compound is a transposed reduced clause: . . . *are oriented towards their peers.*

S3 *having* – This is another instance of the present participle of a stative verb, implying reason or cause.

S4 *choosing* – The present participle here functions as an adjective giving more information about the noun *people; socializing* (in S3) functions in the same way.

S4 *is disappearing* – The time focus (of broad present) is provided at the beginning of the sentence, *these days.*

S5 *this* – That is, the fact (in S4) that the middle child is disappearing.

S5 *some* – This is the beginning of a two-part textual device (the other part being *other* later in the same sentence) that establishes a balance in the last sentence.

S5 *predicting* – Here the present participle functions as an adjective providing information about a noun *(psychologists);* similarly with *fearing* in the same sentence.

S5 *mediating* – Here the participle has an object *(influence)* and the whole expression functions rather like an adjective + noun construction. When, as here, the participle precedes the noun (the unmarked adjectival position in English), the inference is that the quality is a permanent rather than a transitory one.

3.14 The gun debate

TOPIC Guns and the law

LANGUAGE POINTS
Complex sentences
Clauses in apposition
Defining relative clauses
Textual cohesion: balanced contrast across sentences

WARM-UP
1 Draw a gun in the middle of the board and brainstorm the subject of guns.

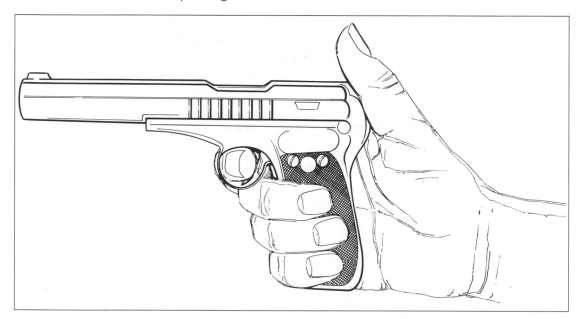

2 Conduct a class referendum. Ask the students:

– *Should guns be banned: yes or no?*

3 If time allows, and feelings are running high, divide the class into two groups, those who said 'yes' and those who said 'no'.

4 Ask each group to co-author a communiqué stating their views (limit the statements to four or five lines).

5 Each group may wish to post their manifesto on the wall of the classroom.

PRE-TEXT VOCABULARY
debate *(n)* discussion of different opinions
to ignite *(v)* to set on fire
to ban *(v)* to bar, forbid, make illegal
firearm *(n)* any type of gun
to seek *(v)* to try to find
compromise *(n)* a midway position that settles an argument
escalation *(n)* a steep increase

TEXT

1 The gun debate, like most controversial and topical issues, tends to ignite passions and drive people into opposing camps.   **2** On the one hand, we have those who believe that when a government bans firearms, it overturns the citizen's most fundamental right, the right to defend self, family, and home against violence.   **3** On the other hand, we have those who believe that the rising incidence of crime and violence is directly related to the ease with which guns may be obtained.   **4** It is in the interests of any reasonable government to seek a compromise between these opposing views, one that allows for the protection of the individual while also preventing an escalation of criminal violence.

NOTES

S2 *on the one hand* – This is the beginning of a balanced contrast that is completed in S3 with *on the other hand*.

S2 *we have* – Or *there is*.

S2 *those* – That is, *people*. There is a comparable construction in S3.

S2 *who believe* – This is a defining relative clause. There is a comparable construction in S3.

S2 *that when* – *That* is the beginning of a noun clause after *believe*; *when* begins a subordinate adverbial clause within the noun clause.

S2 *it* – That is, the *government* just referred to.

S2 *the right to defend* – This is a clause in apposition to the noun *right*.

S2 *self, family, and home* – The definite article *the* could be used here: *the self*.

S3 *believe* – This verb once again generates a noun clause: *that the rising incidence*.

S4 *it is in the interests of* – Or more directly and less formally, *governments should*.

S4 *one that* – This is a clause in apposition to the antecedent, *compromise*.

3.15 Teen suicide

TOPIC

Adolescence
Death

LANGUAGE POINTS

Connectors
Articles: definite, indefinite, and zero
Textual reference

WARM-UP

1 Write up the two topic areas of the title on the blackboard.

2 Conduct a prediction exercise. Elicit from the class any ideas that might predictably be included in the text.

3 Write these ideas as brief headings on the board. Then mark the ones that have been predicted successfully.

4 Next, add any important omissions from the list that, if known to the students, would help them in the dictation.

5 Allow a discussion to flow on any of the issues arising from the topic of 'teen suicide' that the students wish to take up.

PRE-TEXT VOCABULARY

source *(n)* origin
concern *(n)* worry
to attribute *(v)* to consider something as a cause
to perceive *(v)* to understand, interpret
trend *(n)* tendency or movement in a certain direction
injury *(n)* hurt, harm, damage

TEXT

1 Teen suicide is an increasing source of concern in today's society.   **2** Health professionals attribute it to a reaction to unresolved conflict within the family and to stress, both real or perceived.   **3** Over the last twenty years the incidence of suicide among teenage boys has doubled, while that for girls has fallen. **4** This trend is explained in two ways, one quite immediate and objective, the other more interpretive.   **5** Firstly, there is the fact that boys usually choose more violent ways of killing themselves. **6** Secondly, among broken families, where the children usually stay with the mother rather than the father, the loss of a father makes a greater impact on a boy than a girl, leading to a greater probability of psychological injury.

NOTES

S2 *it* – That is, *teen suicide.*

S2 *to* – This preposition follows *attribute*. In this sentence there are two indirect objects (*conflict* and *stress*) both of which are connected to the verb *attribute* by the preposition *to*.

S2 *both real and perceived* – This phrase is in apposition to *stress*.

S3 *over the last twenty years* – This time focus – past continuing into present – requires the present perfect tense, as witnessed in *has doubled* and *has fallen*.

S3 *that* – This substitutes for (and hence avoids the repetition of) *the incidence of suicide*.

S4 *in two ways* – This expression is then amplified: *one . . . the other*.

S5 *firstly* – This refers back to *one quite immediate and objective* in S4. Similarly, *secondly* in S6 refers back to *the other more interpretive*.

S5 *the fact* – This also links up with S4 *the one quite immediate and objective*.

S6 *where* – Or *in which*.

S6 *the mother . . . the father* – *Their* could be used instead of *the*.

S6 *leading to* – This participial phrase could be replaced by a second finite clause: *and this leads to*.

3.16 Calling non-sleepers

TOPIC

Human behaviour
Sleep patterns

LANGUAGE POINTS

Defining relative clauses
Superlatives
Participle clauses

WARM-UP

1 Introduce the topic of sleep patterns.

2 Elicit the kinds of questions you would ask if you were carrying out a survey on people's sleep patterns, e.g.

- *How do you sleep?*
- *How do you get to sleep?*
- *Do you ever wake up during the night?*
- *Do you have difficulty falling asleep or getting back to sleep if you wake up?*

Or see the questionnaire in Maley and Moulding, *Learning to Listen*, p.3.

3 Divide the class into groups according to sleep patterns, e.g. insomniacs, deep sleepers, people who have difficulty falling asleep, but once asleep sleep well.

4 Label parts of the room accordingly.

5 Now ask the students to mix and mingle, asking and answering questions about sleep patterns. Ultimately, everyone should end up in a group of people with similar sleep patterns.

6 Ask the students how it felt discovering other people with similar problems.

PRE-TEXT VOCABULARY

slight *(adj)* very small
to arouse *(v)* to wake
to toss and turn *(idm)* to spend a wakeful, restless night
to seek *(v)* to look for
to wear off *(v)* to stop working or having an effect
insomniac *(n)* a person who has difficulty with sleep

TEXT

1 Are you one of the many who lie awake at night listening to anything that makes the slightest noise?   **2** Or are you aroused from sleep in the middle of the night only to spend the rest of it tossing and turning?   **3** Insomnia is one of the most common yet most misunderstood problems for which otherwise healthy and normal people seek professional help.   **4** Conventional medicine, however, is of limited help: the typical sufferer will be prescribed some form of medication that is effective in the short term, but invariably wears off, leaving the insomniac back where he or she started – desperate for a good night's sleep.   **5** In recent years, in an effort to remove the cloud of mystery surrounding insomnia, researchers have invited insomniacs to volunteer in treatment programmes so that their sleep patterns and behaviour can be studied.

NOTES

S1 *the many* – That is, *the many (people)*.

S1 *who lie awake* – The relative pronoun *who* begins a defining relative clause providing essential information about the antecedent *many (people)*.

S1 *listening* – The present participle begins a participle clause that is adverbial in function adding meaning to the verb *lie awake*.

S1 *that makes* – The relative pronoun *that* begins a defining relative clause providing essential information about the antecedent *anything*.

S1 *slightest* – This is the superlative form of the adjective *slight*.

S2 *it* – That is, *night*.

S2 *tossing and turning* – These present participles function as object complements of the verb *spend*.

S3 *most common . . . most misunderstood* – These adjectives are both in the superlative form.

S3 *otherwise* – This is an adverb lending further meaning to the adjective *healthy*.

S4 *however* – This discourse marker indicates a forthcoming contrast to the previous sentence.

S4 *the typical sufferer* – This is the generic form. It occurs later in the same sentence in the form *the insomniac*.

S4 *leaving* – The present participle begins an adverbial participle clause.

S5 *surrounding insomnia* – This participle clause has an adjectival function adding meaning to *cloud of mystery*.

S5 *so that* – This is a clause of result, linking the action (an invitation to insomniacs) with the expected result (a study of their sleep patterns).

3.17 Marriage returns

TOPIC

Marriage
Relationships
Society

LANGUAGE POINTS

Conditional perfect tense for speculation about the past
Degrees of certainty
Preparatory subject/object
Prepositional phrase of concession: *in spite of*
Future in the past
Textual cohesion through balanced comparison and contrast

WARM-UP

1 Conduct a class survey on attitudes to marriage. The following questions may help:

– *Do you think that marriage is out-dated (yes or no)?*
– *Why do people get married?*
– *Why do people have de facto relationships?*

2 When you have completed the survey find out how many of your students are married. Of those who are not, how many would like to be?

PRE-TEXT VOCABULARY

liberation *(n)* freedom
so-called *(adj)* so named, perhaps wrongly
de facto *(adj)* in fact though not by law
generation *(n)* 25-30 years
to take for granted *(idm)* to assume, expect, without thinking
role *(n)* the usual or expected part taken in life
bond *(n)* something that joins people together

TEXT

1 In spite of the women's liberation movement and the so-called sexual revolution of the sixties and seventies, and in spite of the increasing number of de facto relationships, it seems that marriage has returned. **2** Recent statistics indicate that the institution has never been so popular. **3** Some things, however, have definitely changed. **4** A generation ago, a couple marrying were younger than today; they probably would not have had sexual relations; and almost certainly would not have lived together. **5** As well, they probably would have taken it for granted that that their roles in marriage were going to be very different. **6** What has not changed, however, is the reason couples give for marrying: as in the past, this continues to be the emotional bond they share and includes the desire for a family.

NOTES

S1 *in spite of* – This is a prepositional phrase which, followed by a noun, has a concessional meaning roughly the equivalent of *although* + clause.

S1 *it seems* – This serves as a preparatory subject for the following clause, *that marriage has returned*. It also serves to reduce the total certainty that would accompany the statement (*marriage has returned*) if it lacked the preparatory subject mechanism.

S2 *the institution* – That is, *the institution of marriage*.

S3 *however* – This indicates that a contrast is being established and suggests that supporting detail will follow.

S4 *marrying* – The participle after the noun serves an adjectival function, giving descriptive information about *couple*.

S4 *were younger* – This statement indicates 100 per cent certainty; *almost certainly* (S4) indicates a little less than 100 per cent; *probably* (also S4) indicates a good deal of surety but less than 100 per cent.

S4 *would have had . . . lived* – Note the use of the conditional perfect (*would . . . have* + past participle) to speculate about the past.

S5 *taken it for granted* – Here *it* is the preparatory object leading up to the noun clause (*that their roles . . . different*).

S6 *what has not changed* – Here *what* means *the thing that*. This 'cleft' sentence construction gives greater emphasis to the real subject (in this case *the reason*) than would exist in a conventionally ordered sentence (subject + verb + complement).

S6 *marrying* – The gerund is used after *for*.

S6 *this* – That is, *the reason couples give for marrying*.

3.18 Life after death

TOPIC

Medical technology
Attitudes to death

LANGUAGE POINTS

Complex sentence construction
Compound nouns
Emphasis indicators
Substitution
Passives

PREPARATION

For this activity you will need to bring to class an organ transplant donor's card like the one below, or, depending on the country you are in, a photocopy of the organ transplant consent section of your driver's licence.

ORGAN TRANSPLANT CONSENT

I hereby consent in the event of my death to the removal of -
* (a) any body organs or tissues;
* (b) the following organs or tissues ....

....

* (Omit if not applicable)

Signature ....

WARM-UP

1 Show your students the donor's card, or the consent section of your driver's licence.

2 Discuss with the class the reasons for having these consent forms and cards (see sentences 3 and 4 of the text).

3 Ask your students whether they would personally pledge their organs or not. This may raise cross-cultural or religious issues. However, if they are prepared to talk about it, encourage discussion that will bring out attitudes to organ transplants.

PRE-TEXT VOCABULARY

futuristic *(adj)* relating to the future

to transplant *(v)* to remove something from one place and put it somewhere else

donor *(n)* a person giving something (an organ, for example)

to pledge *(v)* to promise

organ *(n)* a part of the body with a particular function, e.g. heart, kidney

tissue-typing *(n)* (gerund) matching body tissues

recipient *(n)* a person receiving something (say, an organ)

TEXT

1 Transplant surgery, once only a futuristic notion, is fast becoming a daily event.　**2** For many, however, the bitter reality is a long waiting list, and in the case of heart-lung candidates, most die before a donor appears.　**3** In some countries, the donor shortage problem may be alleviated now that people can pledge their organs after death by signing their consent on their driver's licence.　**4** Although the signed consent gives legal permission for the use of organs, the transplant teams speak to relatives wherever possible before going ahead, partly because the relatives themselves need to understand the situation.　**5** However, the pledge does mean that if relatives cannot be found or do not exist, a person wishing to donate organs can do so legally without depending on others' permission.　**6** Once a possible donor has been found, blood samples are sent to the blood bank to be tissue-typed, the recipient with the closest tissue match is chosen and preparations for the operation are begun.

NOTES

S1 *once only* – That is, *(which was) once only*.

S1 *fast becoming* – The adverb *fast* modifies the verb *become* and takes a mid-position between the auxiliary *is* and the verb *becoming*. Note that the present continuous tense is used here to denote the broad present.

S2 *for many* – *Many* stands for *many people*. See also *most* in the same sentence.

S3 *donor shortage problem* – Note the compound noun construction in which the first two nouns really function as adjectives: *donor* indicates what sort of shortage it is and *donor shortage* indicates what sort of problem it is.

S4 *themselves* – The reflexive pronoun serves to add emphasis to *relatives*.

S5 *the pledge* – That is, *the signed consent on the driver's licence*.

S5 *does mean* – The use of the auxiliary *does* here serves to emphasize the verb to which it is connected.

S5 *can do so* – That is, *can donate organs*.

S6 *found* – The passive voice is used here to give focus to the process. See also, in the same sentence *are sent, to be tissue-typed, is chosen, are begun*.

3.19 Child rationing

TOPIC

Population explosion
The family in China
Government

LANGUAGE POINTS

Participle clauses   Passives
Clauses of cause and result   Complex sentence construction

WARM-UP

1 Brainstorm the subject of China, writing up on the blackboard all suggestions as they are given.

2 When the board is full, circle any words that relate in some way to the concept of China's population explosion.

3 Now ask the class to guess what the connection is between the circled words.

4 Introduce the population problem in China as a discussion point, and steer the discussion towards the main issues covered in the text, for example, the effect of over-population (sentences 2 and 3); rumours about the use of force (sentence 4), and (in sentence 5), how economic coercion works. Try to incorporate some of the actual lexis of the text into the discussion.

PRE-TEXT VOCABULARY

tough *(adj)* harsh, severe
to avert *(v)* to prevent
gargantuan *(adj)* huge, enormous
to keep up *(v)* to progress at the same rate
wake *(n)* following as a result or consequence
breach *(n)* breaking, violation (of a law)
civil rights *(n)* people's basic freedoms
under duress *(idm)* by compulsion, force
coercion *(n)* force
to revert *(v)* to return, go back

TEXT

1 China has adopted a tough family planning policy to avert a population explosion of such gargantuan proportions that it would bring famine in its wake. 2 The Chinese, numbering over a billion, have overcrowded cities, an acute housing shortage, and inadequate medical, social, and educational services. 3 They are periodically deprived of electricity because the supply cannot keep up with the demand. 4 The government's measures for dealing with the situation are said to be in breach of civil rights, with stories of abortions and sterilizations being carried out under duress.
5 The main tool, however, is economic coercion: the subsidy that a one-child family receives is withdrawn if they have another; their wages are cut, their monthly bonuses stopped, and their housing allocation reduced, giving them more children but less space.
6 China intends to revert to the two-child family after the year 2000 but in the meantime, the traditional family structure is being revolutionalized by a generation of one-child families.

NOTES

S1 *such . . . that* – Note the construction *such* (+ adjective + noun) + clause of result (*that it would bring famine in its wake*).

S1 *it* – That is, *the population explosion*.

S2 *numbering* – Or *who number*. Note that the phrase *numbering over a billion* could begin the sentence, preceding the subject *the Chinese*.

S4 *being carried out* – The participle clause suggests a causal connection, that is, the use of force is the reason for the alleged breach of civil rights.

S4 *under duress* – An alternative would be to use the adjective *forced* before *abortions and sterilizations*.

S5 *the subsidy that* – The relative clause here is a defining one as it provides information vital to make sense of the sentence.

S5 *is withdrawn* – Note the passive voice to provide emphasis on the process and the impact on the receiver of the action, that is, the two-child family. There are other verbs in the passive in this sentence, some of which have the auxiliary omitted but understood: *are cut, (are) stopped, (is) reduced*.

S5 *they . . . their* – The pronoun stands for *a one-child family* mentioned earlier in the sentence.

S5 *giving* – Here the participle clause suggests a consequence or result: because the housing allocation is reduced and because they have an additional child, they have less space.

S6 *is being revolutionized* – The present continuous tense is used to refer to the broad present, the durational sense of *these days*.

3.20 Litigation lunacy

TOPIC

The law
People and behaviour

LANGUAGE POINTS

Past perfect tense
Reduced relative clauses
Perfect infinitives
Textual connectors

WARM-UP

1 Introduce the concept of litigation (taking someone to court to sue for damages or compensation).

2 Elicit any experiences that the students may have had or may know about in this regard.

3 Write up the title of the text and ask the students to make predictions as to content. Focus attention on the word *lunacy*.

4 Give some examples of this lunacy such as the five in the text: boy/parent case, prisoner/warden case, ladder/manure case, poodle owner / vet case, and Transport Department case.

5 Use the board to write up cues for the fives cases:

- *boy/parents/$350,000*
- *prisoner/warden/$4.5 million*, etc.

Provide more cues if you think the class need them. The idea is to reduce the burden on short-term memory.

6 Be sure to tell (not read) each of the stories in the manner of anecdotes, answering any questions along the way to ensure that the meaning is quite clear. All this will help make a very long text more accessible during the dictation phase.

PRE-TEXT VOCABULARY

rash *(n)* an outbreak
law suit *(n)* prosecution of a case in a law court
to sue *(v)* to take someone to court for legal action
ludicrous *(adj)* ridiculous
manure *(n)* animal faecal waste
poodle *(n)* a breed of dog
vet *(n)* an animal doctor
a pretty penny *(idm)* a lot of money
to take notice of *(v)* to consider, respect

TEXT

1 The US is experiencing a rash of law suits as people turn to the courts to sue for money as compensation for misfortunes suffered. **2** While this trend may have started out quite legitimately, it has blown up into ludicrous proportions. **3** Recently, for example, a boy sued his parents for $350,000 because he did not like the way they had brought him up. **4** Elsewhere, a prisoner who had had five years added to his prison term because of an attempted escape, sued the warden who was on duty that day for $4.5m. **5** In another case, a ladder manufacturer was successfully sued for $300,000 because a ladder he had manufactured slipped when placed on some wet dog manure. **6** In yet another case, the owner of a poodle sued his vet for $45,000 for psychological damage suffered by the dog following some medical treatment. **7** Another man is suing the Department of Transport for millions of dollars for having lost his driver's licence. **8** There is no doubt that some individuals – and a lot of lawyers – are making a pretty penny out of a legal system that takes little notice of justice and even less of common sense.

NOTES

S1 *is experiencing* – The present continuous tense is used to denote an action that is happening in the broad present (*these days*). See also *is suing* (S7) and *are making* (S8).

S1 *as* – Here *as* has either a causal meaning (accounting for the *rash of law suits*) or a sense of simultaneity (the rash of law suits is occurring while people are turning to the law for compensation).

S1 *to sue* – This is the infinitive of purpose providing a reason for the previous verb *turn to*. Note *sue* + object (that is, the person/institution being taken to court) + for (+ money).

S1 *misfortunes suffered* – That is, *misfortunes (that have been) suffered*. There are a number of examples of reduced relative clauses in this text (see *when placed* (S5), *damage suffered* (S6)).

S2 *while* – The sense here is concessional: *even though*.

S2 *may have started out* – The modal *may* + perfect infinitive *(have started out)* is used for speculating about what possibility has happened in the past.

S3 *had brought him up* – The past perfect tense is used to indicate that this action (the bringing up of the boy) preceded the action of the law suit (which takes the simple past tense: *sued*). See also the use of the past perfect tense in S4 *(had had five years added)*, S5 *(he had manufactured)*.

S4 *elsewhere* – This connector serves the purpose of showing that another example follows. Connectors are used through the text as a way of ordering and linking the examples: *in another case* (S5), *in yet another case* (S6), *another man* (S7).

S4 *had had five years added* – This is the past perfect tense of the structure: *to have* + object *(years)* + past participle *(added)*.

S4 *attempted* – This is an example of a reduced relative clause *(that had been attempted)* being transposed to adjectival status and preceding the noun *(escape)* which it describes.

S4 *the warden who* – The relative pronoun *who* begins a defining relative clause that contains information vital to making sense of the sentence. See also S8: *a legal system that*.

S4 *that day* – That is, *the day of the attempted escape*.

S5 *when placed* – That is, *when (it was) placed*.

S6 *damage suffered* – That is, *damage (that was) suffered*.

S7 *for having lost* – Or *for losing*.

S8 *making* – Note the construction: *to make* + money + *out of*.

S8 *little* – Note that the meaning here is negative *(nearly none)* as distinct from the positive, if minimal, meaning of *a little*.

S8 *even less of* – That is, *even less (notice) of*.

Thematic index

This index is included to assist your selection of a text from a thematic or topical perspective. The topics covered are listed alphabetically. Note that the units are listed both by number and by name. The number will give you an indication of level: 1 = pre-intermediate; 2 = intermediate; 3 = post-intermediate/advanced. Within each section (e.g. 1.1–1.20) units are graded according to difficulty. So, for example, in the topic area of *Adolescence* there are three units, 2.6 (low-intermediate), 3.2 (early post-intermediate), and 3.15 (advanced).

Structural index

This index is included to assist your selection of a text from a structural or grammatical point of view. The structures covered are listed alphabetically. Note that the units are listed both by number and by name. The number will give you an indication of level: 1 = pre-intermediate; 2 = intermediate; 3 = post-intermediate/advanced. Within each section (e.g. 1.1–1.20) units are graded according to difficulty. So, for example, in the structural area of *Adverbs* there are three units, 2.5 (low-intermediate), 3.4 (early post-intermediate), and 3.12 (advanced).

Bibliography

Hannan, J. 1989. 'Easing students into Dictogloss' in *TEA News* (Australia), Vol. 7, no. 1. This article explores a number of ways to 'ease' learners new to Dictogloss into the procedure. It is especially valuable for teachers using the procedure with low-level groups.

Llewelyn, S. 'A research project using classroom-based data drawn from classes using Dictogloss' in an unpublished manuscript which is part of her Graduate Diploma in TESOL from the Institute of Technical and Teacher Education (ITATE), Sydney.

Llewelyn, S. 1989. 'The dictogloss procedure and grammatical consciousness-raising: classroom-based research' in *Prospect* (Australia), Vol. 5, no. 1. This article centres on the debate about the place of grammar in language learning. It contrasts the 'non-interface position' (where grammar is considered a non-helpful part of learning) with the 'interface position' (where explicit grammatical consciousness-raising is seen as advantageous to the language learning of adult students). The place of dictogloss in this debate is considered and the writer argues that the strength of the procedure is that it allows learners to work through grammatical processes. The case is supported by classroom-based research.

A number of articles have been written by Ruth Wajnryb on various aspects of the dictogloss procedure:

1987. 'Creating and analysing text in the Dictogloss method' in *TEA News* (Australia), Vol. 5, no. 1. This article is an account of a workshop conducted in text design for dictogloss lessons. It analyses text for the purpose of highlighting the integral features of 'a good Dictogloss text'. It concludes with a list of key tips and pointers for teachers wishing to design their own texts.

1987. 'Group work in the Dictogloss method – learner involvement and interaction' in *BABEL* (Australia), Vol. 22, no. 2. This article looks at the nature of group work and peer interaction in dictogloss and relates this to recent research into task-based group activities in language learning. Nine aspects of group work are closely examined and the various advantages analysed.

1987. 'Myths and Fallacies – common misconceptions about the Dictogloss method' in *Interchange* (Australia), no. 10. This article examines five misconceptions about dictogloss and sets the record straight in terms of what the procedure aims to achieve. These areas of interest are: the relationship to the teaching of listening and note-taking, the place of memory, the question of whether the procedure is success or failure oriented, and the place of grammar.

1988. 'The Dictogloss method of language teaching – a text-based, communicative approach to grammar' in *English Teaching Forum*, Vol. 26, no. 3. This article has its focus on procedure and outlines the basic steps involved. It serves as a good introduction to the reader who is unfamiliar with the process of a dictogloss lesson. It also attempts to accommodate this procedure for teaching grammar into the broader framework of approaches to grammar in the EFL/ESL classroom.

1988. 'The information gap – the role of memory and creativity in the Dictogloss method' in *RELC Guidelines* (Singapore), Vol. 10, no. 1. A key feature of dictogloss is the dictation phase during which, because of the speed of the reading and the density of the text, learners manage only to produce a fragmented text where the essential cohesion is missing. This is 'the information gap' that exists at the heart of a dictogloss lesson. This article explores the implications of this information gap for the roles of memory and creativity in the reconstruction process.

1988. 'The theoretical bases of the Dictogloss procedure of language teaching' in *ATESOL* (Australia) Occasional paper, no. 5. This long article examines the various theoretical bases that underlie the procedure and success of dictogloss. It looks in turn at the psycholinguistic, linguistic, psychopedagogic, methodological, and cultural base of dictogloss. The article is intended for a reader already familiar with the actual procedure and is keen to explore and understand it at a more theoretical level.

1989. 'Dictogloss, teacher-proofness and Murphy's Law'. Proceedings from the 6th ATESOL Summer School (Sydney, Australia). This article looks at the concept of teacher-proofness, or self-sufficiency in methodology, in relation to dictogloss. Using the Teacher-Proof Scale as a measuring instrument, it is suggested that dictogloss is rather low on the scale, requiring relatively high dependence on teaching skills. Five separate features of dictogloss are targeted for discussion: the teacher's grammatical knowledge; the teacher's ability to design a good text; the teacher's managerial skills in facilitating group work; the teacher's ability to pitch the lesson to the level of the target group; the teacher's skill in explaining the methodology to the learners.

1989. 'Dictogloss: a text-based approach to teaching and learning grammar' in *English Teaching Forum*, Vol. XXVII, no. 4, October. The dictogloss text is a pedagogic tool harnessed in the classroom for speficic objectives. This article explores the criteria underlie the creation for effective dictogloss texts.